USE
THE
FORCE

USE
THE
FORCE

A JEDI'S GUIDE TO
THE LAW OF
ATTRACTION

JOSHUA P. WARREN

Aadamsmedia

AVON, MASSACHUSETTS

Published by
Adams Media, a division of F+W Media, Inc.
57 Littlefield Street, Avon, MA 02322. U.S.A.
www.adamsmedia.com

ISBN 10: 1-4405-8685-3
ISBN 13: 978-1-4405-8685-9
eISBN 10: 1-4405-8686-1
eISBN 13: 978-1-4405-8686-6

Printed in the United States of America.

10 9 8 7 6 5 4 3 2 1

Library of Congress Cataloging-in-Publication Data

Warren, Joshua P.
  Use the force / Joshua P. Warren.
    pages cm
  Includes index.
  ISBN 978-1-4405-8685-9 (pb) -- ISBN 1-4405-8685-3 (pb) -- ISBN 978-1-
4405-8686-6 (ebook) -- ISBN 1-4405-8686-1 (ebook)
  1. New Thought. 2. Vital force. 3. Success. I. Title.
  BF639.W325 2015
  158--dc23
                                              2015006536

This book is available at quantity discounts for bulk purchases.
For information, please call 1-800-289-0963.

Dedication

In remembrance of my friend and mentor, Charles A. Yost. He was a wizard of science and exploration who told me the meaning of life is *to learn*.

Contents

Introduction

"Feel. Don't think. Trust your instincts."

—Qui-Gon Jinn to young Anakin, *Episode I: The Phantom Menace*

As of this moment, your life will never be the same. *You* are ready to become a *true* Jedi. Regardless of whether you don a flowing cloak or pick up a buzzing lightsaber, this book will teach you how to actually, realistically use the Force to dramatically improve your finances, health, and relationships by controlling the reality around you. The information in this book is incredibly powerful, proven, and surprisingly simple to apply. It's right at your fingertips. Just wave your hand to turn each page. It is no coincidence that you are reading these words right now. We have probably never met in person, but I have attracted you, and you have attracted me for a reason.

You want the same thing I want—the same thing *everyone* wants . . . a fun, rewarding life and peace of mind. Many consider these things unobtainable, but by the time you finish reading this book, you will have the power to attain them. Believe it or not, you can be a *true* Jedi. In fact, this book exists because I attracted the right publisher. After we made a deal, I learned the publishing staff had decided to attract a book like this. Surely, we were all meant to come together and share in this message at this time.

In his book *Morals and Dogma*, philosopher Albert Pike says, "Think only that if some single law . . . were at once repealed, that of attraction or affinity or cohesion . . . the whole material world . . . would instantaneously dissolve, with all Suns and Stars and Worlds throughout . . . into a thin, invisible vapor."

There is a real and tangible force that holds all of reality together. Once you are able to understand its mysteries, you can direct and shape it. You will be able to reform the world around you to your liking.

If you have any doubt this force can be used to produce extraordinary success, look at the man who incorporated this philosophy into his films. George Lucas was twenty-nine years old in 1973 when he signed the official deal to write and direct his creation, *Star Wars*. He received just $150,000. The spiritual tone of the movie resonated with viewers around the world, and it became the highest-grossing film in history at that time, earning more than $460 million in the United States and $314 million overseas. Lucas went on to become one of the most financially successful filmmakers of all time. As if the astonishing success of *Star Wars* wasn't enough, he also invented Indiana Jones, spawning another of cinema's most famous and successful franchises. Today, *Forbes* estimates George Lucas's wealth at more than $4 billion, an amount more than the yearly budget of some American states. Though there are things in life more important than money, this figure reflects the appreciation of people around the globe for one man's work.

I have spent more than twenty years traveling the world investigating mysterious and metaphysical phenomena. Regardless of the subjects I explore, each time the data leads me back to human perception. The interplay between you and your environment is a dynamic loop. As the nineteenth-century American author Charles Fort said, "One measures a circle, beginning anywhere." Humans are not just passive subjects of an uncontrollable reality but are extremely active co-creators, sending back signals that determine how the next moment unfolds.

The concepts in this book incorporate the essence of the world's most effective spiritual and mystical philosophies and traditions. By placing them in the context of the Star Wars paradigm, we can appreciate them from a fresh, modern perspective, more relevant now than ever.

The facts are this: You were born a creator. You *are* a creator. You are creating right now. You have no choice but to constantly, automatically, and involuntarily create something each and every moment of your life.

The purpose of this book is to show you how incredibly simple it is for you to become a master of this creative ability, harnessing it to improve your life dramatically, starting this instant. You must clear your mind, trust in the wisdom, and prepare yourself to learn.

This book is called *Use the Force*. The most important word in the title is *Use*.

Chapter One

What Is It?

"The Force is what gives a Jedi his power. It's an energy field created by all living things. It surrounds us and penetrates us; it binds the galaxy together."

—Obi-Wan to Luke, *Episode IV: A New Hope*

In 2005, Steve Silberman of *Wired* magazine asked George Lucas about the origin of "the Force." Lucas responded, "Similar phrases have been used extensively by many different people for the last 13,000 years to describe the 'life force.'"

But what exactly is this "force"?

Furthermore, how can the Force work for you?

Like Attracts Like

In the late 1800s, mystic writers such as Madame Blavatsky began using the term "Law of Attraction" in reference to the relationship between matter and energy. Other writers in the early 1900s clearly defined this phrase as a simple, yet profound concept: *"Like attracts like."*

In 1909, English writer Thomas Troward stated it more eloquently: "The action of Mind plants that nucleus which, if allowed to grow undisturbed, will eventually attract to itself all the conditions necessary for its manifestation in outward visible form."

Ultimately, your physical reality is literally flexible. You can actually bend the world into the experience you want to have by shaping your own thought patterns. The Force is the Law of Attraction.

Determine Your Reality

In *Episode I: The Phantom Menace*, Qui-Gon Jinn kneels down before a young Anakin Skywalker, looks him in the eye, and passes along this heartfelt wisdom: "Always remember, your focus determines your reality." When Anakin's focus eventually becomes consumed by hatred, he morphs a dark and suffering world around himself, transforming into Darth Vader. What do you want *your* reality to be?

- Do you want to be rich?
- Do you want a new house?
- Do you want a new car?
- Do you want the perfect lover?
- Do you want better health?

These are all things that you can achieve, with relative ease if you understand how to use the Force. You can make it work for you as you follow some basic, steadfast rules.

This book is designed to teach you step by step how to make the Force, this Law of Attraction, work for you. You should be excited right now, since no matter what challenges you face or how giant your dreams, the Force is powerful enough to make your wishes come true.

If you have any doubts about the practical aspects of how this can change your life, just read these actual quotes from some of the world's most successful people:

"Whether you think you can,
or you think you can't—you're right."
—Henry Ford

"What you focus on expands, and when you focus on the goodness in your life, you create more of it . . . You don't become what you want, you become what you believe."
—Oprah Winfrey

"The people who are crazy enough to think they can change the world are the ones who do."
—Steve Jobs

"I've always believed in magic. When I wasn't doing anything in this town, I'd go up every night, sit on Mulholland Drive, look out at the city, stretch out my arms, and say, 'Everyone wants to work with me. I'm a really good actor. I have all kinds of great movie offers.' I'd just repeat these things over and over, literally convincing myself that I had a couple of movies lined up. I'd drive down that hill, ready to take the world on, going, 'Movie offers are out there for me, I just don't hear them yet.' . . . Intention is everything."
—Jim Carrey

"You create your own universe as you go along."
—Winston Churchill

"If you can dream it, you can do it."
—Tom Fitzgerald, Disney Imagineer

"Imagination is everything. It is the preview of life's coming attractions."
—Albert Einstein

"When one door of happiness closes, another opens; but often we look so long at the closed door that we do not see the one which has been opened for us."
—Helen Keller

> "I have decided to be happy,
> because it's good for my health."
> —Voltaire

Be a Jedi Master

It's possible these figures are what we might call the *Jedi*. A Jedi is, simply enough, an expert in use of the Force. George Lucas was a fan of Japanese movies showcasing the Edo Period, from 1603 to 1868; in these films samurai, farmers, and craftsmen are embroiled in epic sagas and adventures. These are period dramas, and the Japanese word for "period drama" is *jidaigeki*. While in Asia, Lucas became familiar with the term and was inspired to call his fictional warriors "Jedi."

The Jedi Religion

In 2001, the term "Jedi" took on a more realistic meaning. An e-mail campaign urged people worldwide to list their religion as "Jedi" on census forms. Hundreds of thousands around the globe obliged, mostly to poke fun at the government. However, this sparked the creation of sincere Jedi religions that have rallied for legislative recognition in countries like the United States, UK, and New Zealand. Official members take solemn oaths to uphold a balanced life, and sometimes end up in the headlines for refusing to remove their hoods or mock lightsabers. In 2009, a twenty-three-year-old named Daniel Jones was ejected from a supermarket in Wales when he insisted on keeping his hood on. The store owner said, "Obi-Wan Kenobi, Yoda, and Luke Skywalker all appeared hoodless without ever going to the dark side, and we are only aware of the Emperor as one who never removed his hood."

Regardless of how one interprets the Jedi philosophy, the impact of the Force has clearly made a powerful impact on pop culture and some human behavior.

Use the Force

The idea of the Force and the comments by successful people may sound intriguing and inspirational, yet you still might have doubts that this can really make *your* life so much better. Fortunately, we have some practical, tangible examples of how and why the Law of Attraction and the Force seem to work.

Everything in the known universe exists in a state of vibration. This vibration can create and influence physical forms. In fact, if you place a sheet of paper on top of an audio speaker and sprinkle a layer of sand over it, that sand will snap into a variety of beautiful, organized patterns when you play certain tones. When the tone stops, the sand falls back into a random, disorganized spread. This not only functions on a two-dimensional scale, but works equally well creating three-dimensional forms when applied to semi-liquid substances. The study of how these resonant vibrations create and hold physical forms is called *cymatics*. It demonstrates that by altering a frequency, we can alter and manipulate the physical activity around it.

Creating Good Vibrations

One of the most organic ways to create a clear, single, well-defined vibration is by striking a tuning fork. Tuning forks are usually made of steel. When you strike the prongs of the fork, a pure, musical tone resonates in the air, and the pitch of that tone is determined by the length and mass of the prongs.

Let's say you are holding a tuning fork in the key of C. In front of you is a row of seven tuning forks in the keys of A, B, C, D, E, F, and G. If you strike the C fork in your hand, amazingly, the other tuning fork in the key of C will also begin to vibrate, even though there is no physical contact between them. The other forks will not react. There will only be an energetic connection between the two forks of the same frequency. This is a very basic form of broadcasting, and it shows that when one tone is activated, a corresponding tone in the surrounding environment responds. If we imagine the tuning fork in your hand as a conscious being, from its point of view it released a vibration to the universe, and a corresponding vibration was returned.

Luke and Leia always shared a strange telepathic connection. In *The Empire Strikes Back*, after losing his hand in a fight with Vader, Luke hangs from flimsy metalwork above a vast drop of certain death. He calms himself, then reaches out with his mind to Leia. She instantly responds and orders Lando Calrissian to turn the *Millenium Falcon* around so they can rescue him. This occurs before Luke and Leia learn they are brother and sister. The genetic similarity they share assists in the effective telepathic transmission between them. It's no different than the uncanny connection mothers often have with their children, regardless of the physical distance between them, especially when a child is in harm's way.

But if you can tune and control the thoughts you radiate, this influence can even extend to seemingly inanimate objects and conditions in your environment. This instant connection between two apparently separate objects in space seems magical. It is exaggerated in the movies when we watch Luke Skywalker concentrate as his lightsaber zips through the air into his hand. Master Yoda used the same process to lift Luke's entire spaceship from the swampy Dagobah muck. In this case, size obviously does not necessarily matter. If the Force can hold the universe in place, it can affect any object in it.

Your Mind As a Tuning Fork

Your mind is just like the tuning fork we spoke of earlier. Whether you like it or not, your mind is sending out vibrational tones to the universe this very second. That means you are constantly creating and influencing the forces and energies that are radiating back toward you. If you release stray thoughts, often filled with doubts and a sense of frustration and negativity, this combination of energies will swirl back around you. As stated scientifically in Isaac Newton's Third Law of Motion, "For every action there is an equal and opposite reaction." So why on earth would anyone intentionally project "bad vibes," since this always results in self-sabotage? In fact, most people do it all the time without ever even realizing they do it! There is a good reason for this.

You've probably heard, over and over, that your mind is divided into at least two categories: the conscious and subconscious. Let's review exactly what this means. Your conscious mind is the one actively thinking about these words. However, if we envision your total consciousness as an iceberg, the conscious part is only the small tip sticking up above the surface of the water. The vast bulk of the mass below the water is the subconscious. Right now, the subconscious is regulating your heartbeat, determining when your eyes blink, and regulating millions of other physiological operations that usually go unnoticed. In addition, it is responsible for retaining your memories and ideas, and cross-referencing them for you as you examine the world each moment. This, too, is a process you don't generally notice. And often that's a problem.

Dangers of the Subconscious

Your subconscious mind may be dredging up negative feelings and radiating them to the world, even though you don't consciously mean for this to happen. Sadly, lots of people have dreary childhoods, just like little Anakin Skywalker. As time goes on, they allow their helpless, fearful, and pessimistic feelings to grow, like weeds in a garden. Why is this so common? It's because of our animal instincts.

Despite all our efforts to rise above animals, we still share a lot in common with them. Keep in mind that we're all made of the same carbon-based molecules and cells. Our animal instincts are based on millions of years of struggling to survive in an aggressive, dangerous, dirty world. When a bear kills a person, we don't think it did the deed out of malice, as we might if a human killed another person. We give animals a pass (usually) because they are operating from instinct; humans are supposed to be better. Humans are much more spiritually and intellectually evolved, but we still possess those parts of the brain that trigger brutal, aggressive thoughts attached to survival, pleasure, domain, and ego.

Because humans strive to rise above animal behavior, we still struggle with those deep-rooted biological tendencies. Wookiee-like thoughts of aggression are rooted in your psyche, and you should not feel bad about having them. However, it is now your responsibility to recognize their existence and realize that they are holding you back in life. Feel happy that you are now consciously aware of this. A problem must be identified before it can be solved.

Of course, solving such an deep-rooted problem is much easier said than done. How can you neutralize your instinctual, negative thoughts to ensure that only positive, constructive things are being broadcast from you, and that only positive energy is returned to you? That's what the techniques in this book are for!

The Force is not only a power you can manipulate, but one you can manipulate with *great* specificity. That means you can not only wish for happiness, but influence the way in which that happiness will manifest (such as having a brand-new house or car, or living in a beautiful place, or finding your perfect partner). Once you understand how to use the Force, you can use it over and over again the rest of your life. It is the opening of a fantastic new door.

You will have enormous fun as you learn about these exercises. This information is coming into your life right now for a reason. You have somehow attracted it to yourself. Now let's keep the flow going as you find out where this is leading you next. Steady yourself, young padawan. You are going to be a powerhouse of controlled manifestation, but first, we must clean your mental slate for a fresh start . . .

Chapter Two

Preparing to Use It

"You must unlearn what you have learned."

—Yoda, *Episode V: The Empire Strikes Back*

We were born in a scientific age, and the scientific method is an extremely powerful tool. Its focus on empirical data has allowed us to form a more cohesive and homogenous world. You can fly anywhere in a short time and talk to anyone almost instantly, regardless of distance. We have technology that boggles the mind. Yet, this is a double-edged sword. The very same method that has made it easy for you to improve your life is used unscrupulously every day by marketers, advertisers, newscasters, talk show hosts, politicians, and propagandists to make you feel bad. They present a problem or threat, often an unrealistic one, hoping to sway your conduct and persuade you to accept their solution—usually buying a product or supporting a candidate.

The people who are trying to manipulate us understand that ultimately, humans often make profound decisions based on how they feel. In their book *Star Wars and Philosophy*, Kevin S. Decker and Jason T. Eberl point out there is one little-noticed phrase that appears in every single Star Wars movie thus far: "I've got a bad feeling about this." It first occurs in the original film, *Episode IV: A New Hope*, when Luke Skywalker sees the Death Star and Obi-Wan realizes it's not a moon, but a gargantuan space station of the Empire.

Feeling plays such an important role in the movies that "bad feelings" are mentioned not only by Jedi Knights, but by other characters as well (including the gruffly pragmatic Han Solo). This is because feelings form the basis of your relationship to the universe and all within it. Whether or not you realize it, the bad feelings you harbor in your psyche are taking an incredible toll on your life and making it far more difficult for you to manifest good things.

It is only natural for humans to have a vast amount of negative baggage stuffed deep inside our heads. The animal instincts inside us are our primitive fears of being eaten. That's a problem common to most creatures on this planet. Every dark space could hold a predator; every rock or hole or crevice could hide a trap. Our DNA has been sculpted by generations of ancestors who survived because they were acutely mindful of dangers and therefore able to survive long enough to pass on genes. However, we humans have now reached a new phase, never before achieved by life on Earth. We now understand enough about our world to manage most of the threatening elements around us. Why, then, do we still tend to cling to the negative? A lot of it has to do with our upbringing.

Parental Figures

Parents and parental figures strive to make such a powerful impression on their kids that many adults are never able to separate themselves from their offspring, even when it is wise to do so. This connection is so mighty that Lucas uses it as the central issue pushing Anakin to the dark side. As a young apprentice, Anakin is already a slightly reckless and unpredictable figure, but when his mother is kidnapped by Tusken Raiders (also called Sand People), and subsequently dies, he finally snaps. Despite knowing that murder is wrong, he is unable to overcome his blind rage; in its grip he single-handedly murders a whole village of men, women, and children.

Though Anakin's turn to the dark side ironically first emerged from love for his mother, more often than not, parental figures unwittingly insert their stresses and neuroses into us along with love. After all, raising a child to adulthood is no easy task, and parents are frequently in a less-than-joyful mood. What things did your parents always complain about?

- We don't have enough money.
- I can't get out of debt.
- You don't look good.
- You're not smart enough.
- Everybody's corrupt.
- Life is hard.
- Nothing comes easy.
- The country is going to hell.
- The world is a dangerous place.

The list of possibilities goes on and on.

What You're Conditioned to Expect

A while ago, I was at a restaurant and overheard the waitress tell a customer that her entire life, her mother had called her Murphy (a reference to Murphy's Law—anything that can go wrong will go wrong) since bad luck seemed to follow her. Though this may have been intended as a playful gesture on the mother's part, it set up this young woman to expect, and therefore manifest, unpleasant and inconvenient circumstances throughout her entire life.

The Buildup of Negativity

Every single time a person in a position of authority made a negative comment around you, it registered permanently somewhere in your mind. Now, after all these years, a plaque of negativity has formed. As with all bad things in life, no matter how harsh, one exposure probably will not do extensive damage to you. However, repeated exposure creates structures of belief.

I am reminded of how a 3D printer works. Each time the cartridge passes a spot, it only delivers one thin layer of substance. However, little by little, as that same point is passed again and again, it eventually grows into a form. The form's size is limited only by the size of the printer that creates it.

If you combine your biologically inherited fear with the negative reinforcement from your parents, and enhance that with daily input from media that presents you with a world filled with problems, your subconscious mind is filled with stuff to make you feel bad. Since you have no choice but to project what's inside to create your outward reality, guess what you are creating? Yes, it really is a self-fulfilling prophecy.

I have worked in the media for many years in a variety of roles. One of those was part-time host on a political drive-time talk radio show. After years of this, I was amazed by how stressful it became to listen to people fight, argue, and insult each other every day. It was even worse to keep up with the news, constantly thinking about bad things as soon as I got up each day. After all, most of the news is considered *news* because it's bad. Therefore, it gives you an extremely skewed version of what's really happening around the world each day.

I finally stopped hosting the political talk show, and stopped even paying that much attention to the news. I got a residence in Puerto Rico, right on the beach. For weeks at a time I would not watch any news or discuss anything political. It was very enlightening. Sometimes, when you turn off the TV and radio and put away the cell phone and computer, you notice the birds are chirping outside happily, the breeze is blowing gently, and the real world you're standing in is much, much nicer than the mental world you've invited into your mind. Maybe that's why Ben Kenobi finally retired as a hermit on Tatooine—to get away from it all. In my travels, I have found most people in the world to be nice and helpful. Most of the streets in the world are safe. The more I expect that, the more I find it.

This brings us to point number one in the process of preparing yourself to use the Force.

Feel Good

Stay away from things that make you feel bad—especially people, even friends or family, who continue to pursue you with their negative thoughts, even if they make you feel guilty for not continuing to subject yourself to their negativity. Just stay away and do not communicate with them, period. Later, we will explore ways to deal with them if you absolutely must.

In the Hawaiian philosophy known as Huna, an oft-cited tenet is that *energy flows where attention goes*. Pause and think about that for a moment. What a wonderful concept this is! This means that you can instantly have control over other things based on the degree to which you think about them. You give some power to anything that enters your mind, and you deny that power to those you ignore.

One great thing about remembering that *energy flows where attention goes* is that you can use it very much like the ol' Jedi mind trick. This ability first appears in *Episode IV: A New Hope* when Obi-Wan famously uses it on a stormtrooper searching for C-3PO and R2-D2. "These aren't the droids you're looking for," he says. The stormtrooper mindlessly parrots back the phrase and allows them to "move along." Obi-Wan then explains to Luke, "The Force can have a strong influence on the weak-minded."

In a similar fashion, you can often sway the direction a conversation will go by selectively addressing only those things a person says or does that you want to reinforce, and ignoring everything else. This is not to suggest that you move through life like a foolish ostrich burying its head in the sand. But you should be much more selective of whom you will converse with. Once the conversation begins, focus on the points of the dialogue that you will allow to advance.

Even if you're not interacting with another person, the principle holds true. At this crucial period when you are clearing your mind to begin using the Force, you must only pay attention to things that strengthen you and avoid anything that makes you feel physically or mentally weaker.

Dealing with the Negative

Winding down and cutting off negative input is like putting on a tourniquet to help taper off the bleeding. However, your next step is to deal with all the dark stuff that is already inside, doing nothing good for you, taking up space that should be filled with happiness. Believe it or not, getting rid of the bad stuff that has nested, or even festered, for years is much easier than you may think. There is a simple technique to accomplish this.

No matter what a person or thing has done to hurt you, scare you, or anger you in the past, it is your memories that continue to harm you. The mind is ultimately unable to distinguish between the inner and outer worlds. For example, if someone you dislike is suddenly standing in front of you, you will probably feel the same way as if that person's name came up in your presence—even if you haven't encountered her for years. That is because your entire world *exists in your mind.*

It doesn't matter if there's a planet out there somewhere made of cotton candy where I can ride a unicorn. If I don't know about it, it doesn't exist in my world. However, because your world is in your head, that makes it easy for you to mentally change your world from a place full of aggressive obstacles to an open fantasy of brimming possibilities. Since we will receive what we send out, it is important for us to only send out good, positive vibes to the universe. Thus, we must neutralize the negative.

The Power of Love and Forgiveness

Of all the things you can do in the universe to neutralize bad things, the most powerful is to use three simple words: "I love you." Those words, even if spoken insincerely at first, carry such psychological weight they can wipe out the dark energy of anything that plagues your mind.

To deal with bad memories, make a list, writing down each unpleasant thing from your past that you can remember. Then, one by one, go down that list and say "I love you and I forgive you" to each one of those things. You may recoil at this idea, but let me further explain.

If justice can be done, and still needs to be done for those who have wronged you in the past, then you can still allow for this. But saying "I love you and I forgive you" actually has nothing to do with their fate. This is about *you*—what is inside your head—and letting you move on so that from now on you only send out positive energy for yourself.

I have always found Proverbs 25:21–22 in the Bible interesting: "If your enemy is hungry, give him food to eat; and if he is thirsty, give him water to drink; For you will heap burning coals on his head, And the Lord will reward you."

When you write out a list of all the things that have made you feel bad, you may cry. That is okay. Get it out. But once you look at each one and say "I love you and I forgive you," you can move on with your life. You've determined that from that point forth the negative energy those memories have had will *no longer* have power over you. Pity those who are so stupid, ignorant, and evil as to hurt others. This exercise will allow you to escape from their crude and brutal tentacles.

As you do this, do not forget to also forgive *yourself*. This can be the most difficult thing to do, but it is no different than forgiving others. We are all human, and we all err. Your future begins now. The past is beyond your control, but the future depends on what you do this very moment. Love and forgive everyone and everything, including yourself, so that your mind can now move on with a clean slate.

In *Episode VI: Return of the Jedi*, Darth Vader's shuttle lands on the Death Star and he chastises an officer for making slow progress. "The Emperor is not as forgiving as I am," he says. Ironically, at the end of the movie, it is a defeated Vader himself who needs forgiveness. As he lies dying, after having saved his son, he says to Luke, "You were right about me. Tell your sister . . . you were right," and then he dies. Despite all his evil deeds, Luke has forgiven his father and burns his corpse with honor.

As the old adage goes, *two wrongs do not make a right*. Just because you have been hurt, that does not mean harboring hurtful feelings will do you any good. Justice will be done in the universe, and those who have done wrong will pay. But do not allow your mind to become an incubator for those bad things you have experienced.

Forgiving is a powerful thing you must do for yourself. Then you will be ready to move on, projecting only the positive energy you want and need to flow back into your life.

Chapter Three

Gratitude

"Thank the maker! This oil bath
is going to feel so good."

—C-3PO, *Episode IV: A New Hope*

It is no secret that Albert Einstein used his imagination to change our world in profound ways. He recalled being only sixteen years old, imagining himself chasing a beam of light. This "thought experiment" helped him to grasp, in real-world terms, the relationship between humans and matter/energy in the universe. While still in his twenties, he was recognized as one of the world's leading scientists, and his theories of relativity ushered in a wondrous new era of incredible scientific achievement.

Einstein is often quoted as having said, "I think the most important question facing humanity is, 'Is the universe a friendly place?' This is the first and most basic question all people must answer for themselves."

It doesn't matter what your religion, philosophy, or belief system is—if you want to attract good things to yourself, you must begin by believing that the universe is a friendly place. Even if you don't feel this to be true right now, you must gradually convince yourself this is true. The more you feel it is true, the more it will be true for you.

As the ghost of Obi-Wan tells Luke in *Episode VI: Return of the Jedi*, "You're going to find that many of the truths we cling to depend greatly on our own point of view."

Each day, when you awaken, you must remind yourself of this phrase: *I live in a friendly, supportive universe that loves me, and wants me to be happy and succeed.*

There are many ways of reminding yourself of this. You can write this phrase on a piece of paper and put it in a spot you're sure to notice first thing each day. Or you can use my favorite method.

Remember the Supportive Universe

If you're like me, one of the first things you look at when you awaken, and last things you see before you go to sleep, is your cell phone. Because your phone is an interactive device, when you think about your phone, your mind enters a state that is open to learning. After all, your brain-matter is always willing to be remolded by new sensory input. You can take advantage of this.

Search the Internet for images that represent a "friendly universe" for you. These images can vary greatly from person to person. I especially like one I found of the cosmos forming a smile, as if the universe itself is warmly grinning. You may prefer a more down-to-earth pic, like two puppies playing, or a sunset over your favorite beach, or even a photo of a loved one being happy. Regardless of what you pick, real or fantasy, make sure it is an image that captures a vast part of your heart. This is intended to represent the *entire* universe, so it needs to symbolize the biggest vision of life you have. Then, save this image as the wallpaper on your cell phone.

Once you have chosen an image that will instantly remind you of this friendly universe, the more you can sprinkle it throughout your day, the better. Save it as the wallpaper on your computer. Print it out and tape it in places you will see throughout the day. If someone asks you what it is, you can explain its meaning, but so long as *you* know and understand it, that is what matters most. Every time you see it, regardless of what you are doing, pause, take a deep breath, and go over these words in your mind, or even out loud: *I live in a friendly, supportive universe that loves me, and wants me to be happy and succeed.*

It's okay if you can't remember all of that. At least just recall: *I live in a friendly universe.* This is something you should do every single day for the rest of your life.

Be Grateful

Now, let's face reality: No matter how optimistic you try to be, every day can be a struggle. You do not live in a tiny bubble, and challenges and problems are always apt to arise. So, how can you further convince yourself that you *do* live in a friendly universe? You do that by taking a moment to be grateful.

It is often said that the Law of Attraction is no different from the Law of Gravity. It doesn't matter whether or not you believe in gravity. If you run off a cliff, disbelieving in gravity won't stop you from falling. In that case, the law is a bad thing. However, it is also the Law of Gravity that keeps your feet planted on the earth so you don't go flying off into space. Since the Law of Attraction is constantly working whether you like it or not, it will continue drawing good things to you if you feel appreciative for the good things you already have.

In *Episode III: Revenge of the Sith*, Yoda advises Anakin, "The fear of loss is a path to the dark side . . . Train yourself to let go of everything you fear to lose." Instead of worrying about what you don't have, focus intensely on all the good things that you *do* have.

After you have acknowledged the friendly universe, take a few moments to recount the things for which you're grateful. Nothing is too small. It's always good to start with your health, even if you have health problems. Recount the things that are *not* wrong with you. For example:

- I am thankful to have sight.
- I am thankful to hear.
- I am thankful to smell.
- I am thankful to taste.
- I am thankful to feel.
- I am thankful to have my rational mind.

Then move on to being thankful for this book, or the electricity in your house and workplace, or the food and water you have, or the shelter over your head, or the people who care for you. Be thankful for as many things as possible in your life—no matter how small—and remember, each time you state your gratitude, that many people out there do *not* have this thing.

You can go down your list of thanks silently, in your head, or you can speak it out loud. Whether or not someone is around, it always seems best to speak aloud if you can, since verbal expression adds even more power and distinction to your intention. When you express gratitude, you are attracting more things for which you will be grateful in the future. This is the Force operating at its purest and most powerful level.

Any time you voice positive feelings toward another person, you are not only projecting something real toward them, but also setting up that corresponding frequency to come back to yourself. Throughout Star Wars, each time a character says "May the Force be with you," he or she is officially offering a blessing, no different than a prayer, externalized from the mind.

Be Happy Now

I was born in Asheville, North Carolina, the heart of the oldest mountains in North America and considered by many a major center of enlightenment research. There used to be a club there called Be Here Now. It was named after the bestselling book on spirituality, yoga, and meditation, *Be Here Now*, published by Ram Dass in 1971. As the years have passed, and I have learned more about the forces that attract what you want, I have felt inspired to rephrase this as: Be Happy Now.

Since how you feel this very moment determines the "waves" you are sending out to the universe to be returned to you, the greatest thing you can do is to be happy now without violating anyone or anything, including yourself. The Dalai Lama says, "If a problem is fixable . . . then there is no need to worry. If it's not fixable, then there is no help in worrying. There is no benefit in worrying whatsoever."

Worrying is often the top distraction from gratitude. But, as you can see, there is no logical need to worry. Worry only creates more worry. Gratitude is what brings answers and peace flowing in your direction.

Focusing on gratitude is a much bigger challenge than most would ever imagine. It requires you to stop playing into the hands of those advertisers, friends, and family who are always trying to sway you with threats of hypothetical future consequences. Enjoying all the good things around you, in the moment, solidifies your connection to reality, sending forth those waves that will determine your future.

The ability to focus on the present and its true ramifications is highlighted in the Star Wars saga by Yoda in *Episode V: The Empire Strikes Back*. During Luke's training, Yoda scolds him, saying he has watched Luke a long time and yet, "All his life has he looked away . . . to the future, to the horizon. Never his mind on where he was [or] what he was doing."

This encapsulates one of the most significant aspects of all Force training. You must be capable of stilling your thoughts and using the power of the present. What is inside your mind this very moment is the most powerful tool you have to create the next, immediate moment. In fact, if you have any doubt the lessons in this book can quickly produce positive changes in your life, you should pay more attention to this aspect of the Force than any other.

Stop reading for a moment and reflect on all the wonderful things in your life for which you should be grateful. In doing so, you will *presently* initiate changes that will draw good things. You will see results in your life in just twenty-four hours, if not sooner.

A Liminal Life

In studying the mysteries of the universe, I have inevitably come across the conundrums of time travel. Here is the basic enigma: The past can only be divided from the future by this thing called the present. But what is the present? How long does it last? One second? It can't be one second because even a second has a beginning and an end, meaning there would be a past and future within our past and future, and this doesn't make sense. A half-second then? The fact is that there is no span of time we can define that doesn't include a beginning and an end. Therefore, the present is an illusion. It is a statement of where your mind is, at any particular stage, as it flows along your universal timeline. Your mind is constantly forming the very next instant, which compels the very next instant, and so on. The exact moment of here and now is what anthropologists sometimes call a *liminal* moment.

"Liminal" comes from the latin word *limen*, meaning "threshold." This word is sometimes used by scholars when describing times around Halloween (also known as Samhain) when a grand transition is taking place from one world to another and the two realms overlap, a gray period where they can temporarily interact with each other. The term is more often used when explaining the progress of rituals, be they ancient or modern. When you enter a ritual, you move from an old mindset and then are initiated into a new mindset. The entire process is fascinating because it embodies the moment, or moments, of change that is occurring. Those transition phases are especially powerful, since the events are moldable and can be personalized for the individual in the ritual.

Luke suddenly leaves Yoda on Dagobah to fight Vader in the liminal period of his Jedi training. This culminates in the dramatic face-off of *The Empire Strikes Back* when Vader tells Luke, "The Force is with you, young Skywalker. But you are not a Jedi yet." Vader cuts off Luke's hand before revealing he is actually Luke's father. Luke acquired this important bit of knowledge as a result of abandoning his focus on the liminal period and traveling to Cloud City; the revelation comes at a great price.

In your Jedi training, it is crucial that you do not forget the extreme power of your liminal life. You must remain squarely in control at all times, fully cognizant of the fact that your present mindset is the singular component guiding your life into the next scenario.

Regardless of what you hope to manifest, whether it be a winning jackpot at the lottery, the attention of a person across the room, or an entirely new life for yourself, you can only do so by taking hold of the one particular moment before you. Always, always, *always* focus on gratitude for what you have. Whether you whisper it to yourself or think it over and over again, each time you do so, you will send rewarding waves through the cosmos.

Any time you think to recount your gratitude you should do it, but it is especially important for you to do so at the beginning and end of your day. Right after you remind yourself that you live in a friendly universe, thank that *same* universe for all you have. When your head hits the pillow at night, do the same thing as you drift off in slumber. These things form the framework for your new Jedi life. You will feel a great weight lifted from your shoulders and a new, bright sensation all around you. Others will notice it, too. This is the blank slate, ready for you to write what you really want to occur. This is the fertile plot in which you will now begin to successfully manifest the specifics of your brand-new life. The fun is just beginning . . .

Chapter Four

Visualizing

"Your eyes can deceive you. Don't trust them. Stretch out with your feelings."

—Obi-Wan to Luke, *Episode IV: A New Hope*

There is a very simple experiment you can do that demonstrates how strongly visualization affects the mind-body relationship. You'll need some kind of a pendulum—a string or chain with a small weight on the end. If you only have a necklace, you can probably make it work if the necklace includes a pendant.

Sit and rest your elbow on a table, holding one end of the pendulum between your thumb and forefinger. Let the weighted end dangle a few inches above the table surface. Hold it as still as possible. Next, envision the weighted end swinging back and forth, toward and away from you. Slowly, it will begin to swing, just as you have visualized. Then change directions, imagining it swinging left to right. Again, the pendulum will comply. You can also think of it swinging clockwise, or counterclockwise. To some, this is a wondrous, almost supernatural, demonstration. Scientists call it *automatism*.

Automatism works because of subtle, almost microscopic motions in the muscles that flex without conscious intent. Each time you think of something, but especially if you visualize it, the muscles instantly respond. This means your body is constantly reacting to your mind. The mind and body are in such sync that it does not even require a specific intention to make a particular motion. The body is, in fact, programmed to relay the commands of the mind almost effortlessly.

Mind and World

The mind's effect on the body is quite clear and apparent. But, we must next ask, just how far does this effect extend into the world? The answer to this question is still a mystery. However, there is no doubt that it extends much further than most think.

In my years as a paranormal investigator, I have often lectured on the human bioenergy field. Frequently, I will show how far the field can extend by setting up a device that is sensitive to the electrical energy around a human. Then I will have an audience member walk by the instrument. The electrostatic field alone often extends five to ten feet around a person of average size. It is clear that your presence goes beyond the visible boundary of the physical body. Yet, even if that presence only goes a very short distance, it is still initiating a chain reaction of particles moving and shifting. This entire process begins with the signals that come from your mind.

The power of the mind over the physical world has been a mystery since the dawn of thought. If I wish my arm to move, it moves. Philosophers have long struggled to understand how this seemingly intangible thing—the mind—connects with your physical body. Scientists know the brain sends electrical signals to the body, but they cannot explain how one's conscious desire initates this physical process. Yet it proves that the things you think about do have physical power. Therefore, the images in your mind can, and do, have a dramatic impact on how the world around you behaves. The most amazing part is that, if you repeatedly visualize what you want in life, almost anything can be manifested by you.

- Want a million dollars?
- Want a nice house on the beach?
- Want to take a trip around the world?
- Want to improve your health and relationships?

All these things—anything that is possible within the natural laws that govern the world—can be materialized by you. Lots of people who read about the Law of Attraction make it this far, try to visualize something, and fail to make it occur. At that point they lose hope and growl that this is a bunch of hogwash. What they do not realize is that there are some simple rules you must follow to properly manifest through visualization. Those rules are *extremely* important.

Manifestation Through Visualization

It is easy to look at successful people and call them "lucky." When Luke is training with a lightsaber on the *Millennium Falcon*, he successfully deflects some shots from a small, floating practice drone (a "remote"), even though his eyes are shielded. When the curmudgeonly Han Solo dismisses it as luck, Obi-Wan quickly replies, "In my experience, there's no such thing as luck." Those people who have made great successes of themselves often do so by consciously understanding the simple rules of manifestation. Of course, some are more naturally inclined than others.

Elements of the Basic Technique

Let's go through the main points of how to manifest something. You may want to read through this section several times before attempting the steps.

Take Five

This means you set aside at least five minutes, every day, to envision exactly what you want to occur. In the movie *The Secret*, Dr. Joe Vitale says, "This is really fun! This is like having the universe as your catalog, and you flip through it and go, 'Well I'd like to have *this* experience, and I'd like to have *that* product, and a person like *that*'—it is you just placing your order with the universe. It's really *that* easy."

You should do this at least once per day. I have found it most effective when done just before I go to sleep at night. However, the more often you do it, the better. It also helps to write down what you want in advance, in short, descriptive sentences. It also helps to word them as if your wish is already fulfilled.

For example, you might write about things you don't yet have:

- I am grateful for my new job at a law firm.
- I am excited about my new house in the scenic Swiss countryside.
- I love spending time with my beautiful new girlfriend.
- I am fortunate that my body heals more every day.

Using those sentences as a guideline, envision what you want with as much detail as possible. If you want a Swiss chalet, see yourself pulling up the driveway, getting out of the car, unlocking the door, opening the door, putting your keys on the counter, and pulling back the curtain to soak in the view, and imagine the way the floor feels under your feet as you walk into the kitchen to pour yourself a beverage.

In this rushed day and age of distraction by cell phones and social media, taking five minutes for yourself can seem like a long time, but it is well worth it. It is wonderful to live out your fantasies in your mind. In fact, you'll probably end up spending more than five minutes each day, since envisioning your wish and believing you really will have it makes you feel good.

Emotional Visualization

In order for your manifestations to work properly, you must connect with them by feeling them. To get the most from your visualizations, you should immerse yourself in them, just like a young, unemployed Jim Carrey staring down on Hollywood and feeling the sensations of being a big movie star. The better you feel as you do this, the more quickly things will take shape. It is not the intellectual part of the brain at work here. That part is the fearful, doubting, critical section. Instead, you should be tapping into what makes you uniquely human—your ability to envision detailed scenarios in your life. Instead of thinking about them as happening in the future, feel them happening to you right now. You should try to think of them as things that have already happened for you, and you are remembering them. That's how distinctly you must connect with these things!

Build on Enjoyment

One trick I have learned is to visualize what I want to manifest whenever I am doing something I enjoy. I like to snorkel in tropical waters (one big reason I manifested myself a residence on the beach). Therefore now, when I'm snorkeling, feeling excited as I float around in the warm water, I use that time to visualize what I want to manifest next. You can do this during anything that makes you happy. If you like eating ice cream, visualize while you're savoring a bowl. If you love a particular piece of music, visualize while you're listening to it. If you like to take bubble baths, use that time. The whole purpose here is to associate your visions with positive feelings that will powerhouse your desires into the universe.

Negative thoughts physically weaken us. Positive thoughts strengthen us. Therefore, a negative thought is much weaker than a positive one. This is a good thing, since we can't help but experience bad thoughts flitting through our heads from time to time. Fortunately, so long as you stay focused on the good stuff, the bad thoughts will pale in comparison to the wonderful things you have mentally set in motion. Eventually, those negative impulses will fade away.

Because emotion is *so* important here, you will have much greater success if you focus on the real-world outcome of your manifestation, as opposed to unnecessary, intermediate stages. For example, maybe you want $1 million to buy a nice house. You can work on materializing the money, but why bother? Just jump straight to having the house! Money, in and of itself, is just a medium for attaining your goal, and it's actually difficult for your brain to attach strong feelings to a dollar amount unless you clearly know what you will do with it. The thing you will ultimately purchase with the money is what will stimulate the emotions to make your manifestation work.

Baby Steps

This entire process is based on the power of your mind, and it's particular to you. It is easier for some people to believe they will own a multimillion-dollar Swiss chalet than others. If, every time you think about having the thing you want, a little voice says, "Come on, honestly! This is a joke. This can never happen to *you*," then you should re-evaluate the incremental steps you are taking to reach your goal.

Do you remember how $100 seemed like an almost unobtainable amount when you were a kid? Then once you finally got a job and earned $100, it became much easier to earn it again. In fact, soon enough $100 seemed like very little, and you next set your sights on $1,000. Once you earned $1,000 it, too, seemed to fly right out of your hands. That's because each time we realize we can achieve something, it makes it easier for us to reach the next level.

The same thing is true of dating. Remember how impossible it once seemed to attract a favorable mate? But once you had one, the process of getting the next one got easier? In fact, this rule can be applied to every aspect of life. Collectors often talk about how their assembly began with one item, yet there was a "Holy Grail" piece somewhere out there that seemed impossible to gain. Eventually, the ones who are serious and persistent finally get what they want.

This shows us that as you start to manifest, you will have more success if you work your way to your ultimate manifestation. If you are used to earning $20,000, it may feel unrealistic to think that you can jump to $1 million. Therefore, instead try to double your income to $40,000, then from there to $80,000, etc. Most people need to apply this gradual scale to everything they manifest. If you don't have a car and need one, try to produce a reliable used car before jumping straight to a brand-new Rolls-Royce. The closer your current state is to what you want, the more quickly and reliably you can attract it to you.

It is common for people who are learning the art of manifestation to start by trying to do very simple things, like to open a parking space on a crowded street in a few minutes. Or if you're in a long line and you want to somehow get through faster, envision it happening. You are learning to speak the synchronistic language of the universe, and it will begin to work with you, opening up opportunities. Every Jedi, no matter how powerful, had to learn and practice, slowly transitioning from altering reality in small ways to commanding the Force. Yet even a great master such as Yoda still had to concentrate to move large objects. There will always be some limits on the mind, but we do not currently know what those limits truly are.

Specific, but Not *Too* Specific

I have stressed the importance of being specific in your wishes. However, in some cases you can be so specific that your wish will not come true, most especially when other living beings—particularly people—are involved. Human energy is extremely complex, and interfering with another's life path can have unforeseen consequences. You should therefore avoid trying to attract a particular person. For example, if you would like an ideal mate, then wish for your ideal mate. Do not, however, wish for a certain individual. You may think someone is perfect for you, but you are not omniscient. The universe is always a much better judge of what is suited to you, and what will satisfy your needs. It is helpful to think of childhood crushes. Maybe, at a certain age, you felt someone would be your dream partner. Ten years later, you looked back with an experienced eye to see this person was not right at all for you.

Or, let's say I think billionaire Mark Cuban would be the perfect business partner for me on a deal. I would be unwise to focus on Cuban. Instead, I should simply try to manifest the perfect partner and allow the natural flow of the Force to sort out the details for me. This is one of the wonderful things about how the entire process works. You don't have to sweat the little details; you just get things going and trust they will work out.

Being too specific also applies to some inanimate objects, as well. If I want an Aston Martin car, I should be able to manifest that. If I want an Aston Martin DB5, that may be slightly more difficult. But if I want *the* Aston Martin DB5 that Sean Connery actually drove in the movie *Goldfinger*, this may be such an impossible goal that it is not worth my time to envision. Always think about getting the most bang for your buck, so to speak.

Time Delay

The moment you project your feelings into the universe, the Force will instantly begin to rearrange itself to eventually conform to your wishes with proper nourishment. However, the universe is a vast place, filled with an unimaginable body of matter and energy. It may seem disappointing to accept you cannot always snap your fingers and instantly materialize whatever you want, but this is actually a very, very good thing!

A large part of the theatrical magic in Star Wars emerges through Jedi sometimes making the world obey their commands in a split second. Whether we watch Obi-Wan or Luke snap a lightsaber into their hands from across the room, or someone spring high in the air like the battling Yoda and Count Dooku, the telekinesis wows us in an action scene. But think of how volatile and dangerous this would be in the real world. What if, in a moment of anger or passion, you choked someone to death remotely, as Vader almost does in *Episode IV: A New Hope*, or, with a wave of your hand, sent someone flying over a cliff or slammed that person violently against a wall? Most humans certainly are not self-controlled and responsible enough to wield such power. Shaping reality in an immense way to conform to our desires requires repeated work, over time, reinforcing your wishes. This still does not, by any means, guarantee that manifestation will not be used for harmful purposes, but at least removes a large portion of rash, impulsive destruction.

Though telepathy plays a small, yet crucial, role in Star Wars, even it is regulated in the films for the same reason. For example, even the Jedi Council cannot simply look into the mind of young Anakin to assess his mental aptitude. They must question him about his thoughts and feelings. I have often felt that if humans had developed the ability to read each other's minds, our race would have destroyed itself long ago! Our civilization is glued together by our abilities to reserve judgment, enjoy private thoughts, and think long-term before taking action on big decisions.

Altogether, the essence of effective visualization is to spend time pretending over and over in your mind that you have what you want, and are simply patiently awaiting its arrival. As you do this, the mind will slowly change from pretend to belief, and this belief will send the strongest signals into the universe, activating a corresponding signal in the Force, transmitting back the things you desire. You are shaping the immaterial mold within which the material will form.

Have you ever paused to consider that every manmade object around you was first simply a thought in someone's head? As James Allen said in his 1902 book, *As a Man Thinketh*, "As the visible world is sustained by the invisible, so men, through all their trials and sins and sordid vocations, are nourished by the beautiful visions of their solitary dreamers."

Effective visualization is the key to using the Force. Throughout the rest of this book, I will clarify the fine points of this powerful skill. As you will soon realize, there is an art to not only projecting your wishes, but successfully receiving them as well.

Chapter Five

Receiving

"If money is all that you love,
then that's what you'll receive!"

—Princess Leia to Han Solo, *Episode IV: A New Hope*

Perhaps the single most underestimated aspect of the Law of Attraction is the simple ability to receive the things you are manifesting. This certainly seems weird and counterintuitive. After all, what's so hard about sitting back and reaping the benefits of your mind power? The problem is that receiving is not simply a passive process. It also takes some effort, and great awareness, on your part.

The things you manifest can only appear by way of the natural laws in the real world. That means, if you wish for a pot of gold, it's not going to simply magically materialize out of thin air and fall at your feet. If only leprechauns were real! You cannot just lazily sit back, relying on your personal gravity alone to attract the grand things you desire. Instead, you must actively participate in the world, expecting to see positive things start to freely appear in your life. Thomas Jefferson is said to have stated, "I am a great believer in luck, and I find the harder I work, the more I have of it." And as the wildly successful Jack Canfield, creator of *Chicken Soup for the Soul*, often says, the last word in "attraction" is "action."

Generally, when you want to materialize something significant and develop the right attitude, you will quickly see signs that your mindset is paying off. Little things will pop up each day. You might find the item you want at the grocery store happens to be on sale that day. Or someone may invite you to go ahead of them in line. Maybe a stranger will give you a nice compliment, or you'll make it back inside your house just before it starts to rain. If you're wishing for financial opportunities, you may literally begin to see money and other valuables lying around. Whenever you see these things, pick them up and take them; accept what's being given, and feel grateful for these gestures of generosity made by the universe. Remember the adage, "Find a penny, pick it up, and all day long you'll have good luck."

Go with the Flow

It is important for you to begin feeling the groove of good things moving your way. Feel lucky. As Obi-Wan memorably advises Luke, "A Jedi can feel the Force flowing through him." A slightly confused Luke asks if it controls your actions. Obi-Wan replies, "Partially, but it also obeys your commands." The point here is that you cannot receive by being passive. You must wade into the world, and go with its flow. The positive things you want will emerge via synchronicities—moments when the various elements of life seem to intersect in your favor, guiding you in a particular direction. Each time this happens, it is a little miracle, and if you follow those miracles, the trail will eventually lead you to exactly what you hoped to ultimately manifest. You may be surprised to see how quickly your life starts improving. This tendency for things to turn your way is perfectly understandable. After all, the Force has *no choice* but to send back to you what you project. Your optimistic mind means good things absolutely must flow to you. Isaac Newton's Third Law of Motion is steadfast: For every action, there is an equal and opposite reaction.

There is no need for you to stress over how your wishes will materialize or guess the exact means. You have no way of knowing precisely what pieces will fall into place, how they will do so, and at what time. This is good news for you, since it means you should relax and just keep an eye out throughout each day. After all, by cosmic standards, it is just as easy for the universe to manifest one cent as it is $1 million. When Luke's X-wing starfighter sinks into the swampy Dagobah sludge, Yoda is disheartened by how quickly Luke becomes exasperated. "Master, moving stones around is one thing. This is totally different," Luke exclaims.

"No!" Yoda corrects him. "No different. Only different in your mind." With that, Yoda proves his point by using the Force to telekinetically lift the heavy craft from the muck.

"I don't believe it," says an amazed Luke.

"That," replies Yoda, "is why you fail."

Feel Abundant

In order to really see the good things flow into your life, you must embrace one extremely powerful belief: *I am surrounded by abundance.* In the same way that feeling you live in a friendly universe sets the stage for your relationship with the Force, feeling you are surrounded by abundance sets the stage for the amount of good things the Force will bring your way each day. This is very difficult for most people, since we are constantly bombarded by the idea of scarcity.

My grandparents lived through the Great Depression. The entire economic collapse of that time was caused by mental recklessness, especially among wealthy stockholders. All economies are based on the minds of the people in charge of the currency. After all, money, as we know it, is not some force of nature that exists apart from humans. We created it, and we also control it. Hence, it is too often just a reflection of human paranoia. Many people constantly associate fear with money. In Tom Shadyac's documentary, *I Am*, scientist David Suzuki says, "A couple hundred years ago, people believed in dragons and monsters. But now we've got another monster, and it's called the economy. And if you read the *Wall Street Journal*, they treat the market and the economy as if they are a thing!"

Because my grandparents were responsible for large families, the scarcity that they experienced poisoned their outlook on life, and they remained afraid the rest of their lives that there would never be enough—even when there was. That shell-shocked belief was inadvertently passed to their children, who in turn passed it to the next generation. The truth, though, is that the world has more than enough of everything for everybody. This is especially true because we all want different things. You might not want my house on the beach, and I might not want your mansion in the snowcapped Rockies. But regardless of whether we're talking about money, possessions, health, or other relationships, we are really just talking about the flow of energy. In fact, money is one of the easiest things to obtain—much less complex than relationships and health. With dollars and cents, it's very straightforward. Money comes from one place: other people. When you do good things that others appreciate, you will be rewarded by the universe. Money equals energy. When you feel abundant and send out the signals of abundance, the universe pours it back to you. Which brings us to another outstanding point: *You must give in order to receive.* This is so important, that it bears repeating: *You must give in order to receive.*

Giving

Have you ever noticed how many rich and successful people always talk about charity? Even President Bill Clinton wrote a whole book simply called *Giving.* Some of the world's richest people, such as Bill Gates and Warren Buffett, inspire other wealthy people to give their money away. Why? And how do those people give so much away yet continue getting richer?

You might be tempted to think that—duh—of course they give money away, because they're rich enough to afford it. Yet, that is not always the answer. Many of the super-wealthy have always believed in charity, even long before they were rich. Often money and resources are given anonymously, or through very personal organizations—for example, tithing to churches. Most of the super-wealthy, successful people in the world understand that the more you give, the more you receive. They understood this early on, and that became the engine that led to their eventual success. From this perspective, giving to others is a self-serving act. Okay, fine then. Everybody wins!

Overattachment to money and other superficial resources is an anchor that will drag you down, restrict your ability to enjoy all of life's wonders, and stifle your freedom. In *Episode I: The Phantom Menace*, Qui-Gon Jinn and his crew are stranded on Tatooine without money to repair their ship. While discussing a way to get help from the unsympathetic locals, Padmé says, "They must have a weakness of some kind."

After learning that gambling is popular in the area, Qui-Gon says, "Greed can be a powerful ally." What he means is that the locals' greed makes them easy to manipulate. A greedy person can be led around by the nose if unhealthily following the prospect of more money.

Han Shot First

In a notable scene in *Episode IV: A New Hope*, Han Solo confronts Jabba the Hutt's henchman Greedo (notice the name!) in the cantina at Mos Eisley. Greedo has come to collect a debt owed to Jabba, and in his haste he fails to notice the latter's blaster aimed squarely at his midsection. In the original 1977 version of the film, Greedo tells Han he's been waiting a long time for this moment. "I'll bet you have," Han replies, and fires his blaster.

To howls of anger by fans, Lucas changed the exchange in the 1997 Special Edition release of the film, making clear that Greedo fired at Han first and Han killed Greedo in response. Hardcore fans of Star Wars took to wearing T-shirts with the slogan "Han shot first." In any case, the message is clear: Greed doesn't pay.

Many wealthy people give their money away because they've always been generous, and they don't need all they have. I understand that it is easy to villify rich people, especially when you hear so much about the 1 percent of the population that holds most of the wealth. But there is a giant difference between wealthy, honest people and those who loot the system at every opportunity.

If you want to receive more money, here is simple trick. Make a decision to give money away that you ordinarily might not give. This may be to a charity, or simply a tip at a meal. But when you do it—and here's the real *trick*—give just enough extra to make you cringe a little. That's right, go just over that edge, out of your comfort zone. A part of you will think, "I am giving too much!" but that's good. That's how you exercise the giving/receiving muscle and expand the net energy flow around you. In the long run, this brings much more money, overall, into your life. Would you rather keep 50 percent of a dollar than have an extra 50 percent of $1,000? Whenever you make a decision to spend money, do so happily and without worry or regret.

In *Episode V: The Empire Strikes Back,* as Han Solo is preparing to make a risky move with his ship, a frightened C-3PO says,

"Sir, the possibility of successfully navigating an asteroid field is approximately 3,720 to 1."

A determined Han Solo snaps back, "Never tell me the odds."

In the spirit of Solo, I would advise you to not let the amount of dollars and cents in your wallet overshadow your instincts. It is foolish to think it is productive and profitable to hoard your money. Go with what you know and what makes common sense. A good friend of mine in Puerto Rico is a Santero, a Caribbean priest of African traditions who practices only extremely positive rituals. He often says that for generations one of the most fundamental tenets of the ancient island religions has been that one must give to receive. Despite this time-proven concept, we live a world where greedy, self-serving attitudes are commonly celebrated in our media. Now, however, you know the true secret to wealth and can see how this secret has been kept for so long, since it's the opposite of how many poor people think. There are stingy rich people, but there are no *happy*, stingy rich people.

I am reminded of a man who won a $20 million lotto in 1996. He was very generous with his money, lavishing gifts on his friends and loved ones. However, his sister-in-law and her boyfriend wanted more. They kidnapped him, initially with a ransom plan. However, things went awry, and they shot him in the head, killing him. These kinds of tragic stories are a plague on many lottery winners. I frequently hear people talk about how their problems would end if only they could hit the lottery. Ironically, the new problems that could arise can be far worse. This scenario also reminds me of the spooky old story "The Monkey's Paw." A poor man is given a magical object and wishes for money. Soon after, his son is killed in an accident, and the father receives as compensation the exactly amount of money for which he'd wished. These kinds of stories remind us that we're not smart or knowledgeable enough to always wish for what is best for us. That is why once you have projected your desire, you must then kick back and allow the universe to step in and determine the best way to deliver it.

How to Receive

The most effective means by which to receive is to feel you are a happy and abundant person. Often, as I take a few moments to meditate on what I want, I close my eyes, use my imagination, and envision myself growing larger and larger, into a gigantic being. As I do this, I will open my arms as wide as possible, assuming the pose of receiving. I am thinking to the universe, "Thank you for your abundance!" As I do this, I feel powerful waves of positive energy flowing through me from this astounding creation. Do not think of money and other wishes only coming *to* you but going *through* you. That way you are a conduit, connected to a constant stream. Don't try to dam the stream. In the same way that it's better to pull a fish from a river than to stop the river from flowing, it's better to draw energy from the positive flow that surrounds you.

The wonderful thing about using the Law of Attraction is that it can help you attain precisely what you want. If you want happiness and peace of mind, you can project that feeling and have the universe provide it for you, without getting in the way of yourself.

I know a lot of people who constantly complain that they never have enough money. Those who are self-employed primarily blame the state of the marketplace (it's not bringing in enough business). Those who are employed by others blame the marketplace for a different reason (raising prices and the high cost of living). Yet, week after week, month after month, these people still somehow manage to get by, and have done so for years. How is this?

Obviously, there is enough money for these folks; otherwise they would not get by. So why do they keep feeling this way? It's because they believe their feelings are caused by the environment. In fact, it's their feelings that *cause* their environment. Once they know they have enough money, something inside them switches off, and they stop properly manifesting more. It is not done consciously, but it is done. If you are able to materialize just enough to get by, then why should it stop there? Shouldn't you be able to continue creating wealth, moving beyond simply having enough and into the realm of true abundance? Having enough allows you to meet your survival needs, but having *more* than enough allows you to have extra money for fun and generosity toward others.

It is very strange to think there is some mechanism inside us that regulates the amount of good things we can have, but that mechanism does exist. It was put in place long ago, programmed into you by your genes, your family, your friends, and much of what we experience through mainstream and social media. Some people have more programming than others, both good and bad. Children of wealthy families have higher odds of growing up wealthy, even if they are not assisted by the family fortune. This is because they have grown up with wealth as a part of their reality. They understand that their mothers and fathers, grandmothers and grandfathers, are not superhumans and are in fact just as flawed as everyone else. That sets up an entirely new mental framework for them. They usually don't even realize they are programmed for wealth more than the rest of us. By the same token, you may not have realized you were programmed to be average, or less. But now you know what is happening. The best part is that you now understand this programming and can change it!

Good and Evil

One thing that is fascinating about the Force is that the Force itself is not necessarily good or evil. It is just a medium, and that medium can be used by any trained Jedi with any intention. The way the Force is channeled and used depends on whether we call upon the "dark side" or the "light," as I will cover in greater depth later. The purpose of this book is not to give the impression there is some sunshine-like energy that you breathe in to solve all your problems. The purpose is to help you understand there is an infinite source of potential energy all around you. When you grasp that, and the fact you can control it, you determine what it will do for you.

The American Film Institute rates Darth Vader as the third greatest movie villain in cinema history, behind Hannibal Lecter and Norman Bates. One of Vader's most interesting lines comes as he uses the Force to choke Admiral Motti: "I find your lack of faith disturbing." This is fascinating since we usually hear the word "faith" only in relation to good and inspirational topics. Obviously, the point being made here is that the Force is impartial. The Force and the Law of Attraction are no more good or bad than the Law of Gravity is good or bad.

It is up to you to be the proper antenna for the Force. You are a transmitter and a receiver. Sending out the transmission begins the process of manifestation, but if you shut down the operation before properly receiving, you have wasted your time. Keep sending out the right signals, but also pay attention when those signals start coming back. This is how you will become part of a harmonic resonance, filling all the space around you with the energy you want, and shifting the matter near you to conform to your wishes. It all sounds wonderful, but I know what you're wondering: *Seriously*, how long is it going to take before my wishes come true?

Chapter Six

Give It Time

YODA: "I cannot teach him.
The boy has no patience."

OBI-WAN: "He will learn patience."

—Episode V: The Empire Strikes Back

Every single manifestation is a unique event. You are a unique person, and you remain unique from moment to moment as you change and age. The thing you want to affect has a unique relationship to you, and that relationship has a unique place in time, constantly altering as minutes, hours, days, and years roll forward. In college, my favorite course was philosophy. I remember hearing, for the first time, the quote of the Greek thinker Heraclitus: "You cannot step twice into the same river." All the variables mentioned here make it impossible to accurately predict exactly when your wish will manifest. But there are many things you should understand to help you gauge timing in your manifestation work.

Once you project a clear thought into the universe, the manifestation begins instantly. Particles of reality begin to reshape and rearrange themselves like grains of sand, slowly being shaken to fall into a new mold. You only get to see the very last stage of a successful manifestation, when it finally materializes. Therefore, the time it takes between the initial thought and the final outcome—be it minutes, days, weeks, months, or even years—can feel frustrating, since the action is taking place behind the scenes. What's more is that during this period you *still* must hold the shape of the mold in your mind, even when you cannot directly see the work taking place. If you forget about it or lose faith in it, then it will fall apart, and your desire will not come to pass. This certainly feels like a big challenge, but it's not if you look at it from a more familiar perspective.

Sowing the Seeds of the Future

When a farmer plants a seed, he buries it out of sight. The farmer has no way of being certain that the seed is undamaged and will indeed grow. Nonetheless, he assumes it likely will, and he treats it well. There are many variables out of the farmer's control, such as weather or wild animals that may disturb the soil. Yet the farmer stays focused on the things that are under his control. He fertilizes the soil, waters the ground, and tends to the land the best way he can. The farmer does not constantly dig up the seed to check and see if it is growing. In fact, if he did so, he would most likely hinder or destroy the seed's progress. With practice and experience, the farmer learns when to expect to see certain stages of development. Of course, it takes less time for an apple seed's sprout to break the soil than it does for that same sprout to grow into a large tree, bearing apples of its own.

No one becomes an accomplished Jedi overnight. Because your varying wishes are so particular to your life, you must learn the rate at which you manifest. Just as Obi-Wan learned under Qui-Gon Jinn and Anakin apprenticed under Obi-Wan, you may also be able to identify successful people in your life who are good at this skill, be they younger or older. If so, tell them you are studying this subject, and ask them for advice on how quickly they have materialized things. I have reached the point where I can usually create a parking space in a few minutes and affect the weather in much less than an hour. I manifested my beach house in a couple months (with the assistance of a Wishing Machine, which I will talk about later), and helped materialize a major TV project in less than eight months. In less than a year, you can turn your entire life completely around and head in a fantastic new direction. But to do so, you must understand some extremely important points.

Repetition

Firstly, *your mind must repeatedly beat a path to your destination*. Imagine you are standing on the edge of a thick forest near your house. You want to reach a cliff, on the other side of the woods, from which a breathtaking sunset can frequently be enjoyed. You know roughly where you're going, but not exactly, so you set off on the clearest route you see, beating the weeds and brush out of the way with a walking stick. Over time, whenever you walk down the path you've created, it will become more and more distinct, gradually forming a clear trail. In fact, you will eventually not even need your walking stick to clear the way. This is the exact same process by which one directed thought becomes reinforced, again and again, into a channel carved out to reach your goal.

The key to ensuring your mind shapes your reality with sincere intention is repetition. Just as a blacksmith shapes molten metal by striking at it over and over again, or a sculptor chisels a lump of stone by knocking away piece after piece, you must constantly blast your thoughts like a laser, cutting your mental image into the cosmos. Every time you send forth another wave of your vision, each more detailed than the last, the path to your target becomes clearer and clearer, strengthening your commands as they move more easily through the medium. The process may begin slowly, like starting up the wheels of a train moving a heavy load, but once you get going, the momentum will build and your vision will accelerate with surprising speed. One of life's little tricks is that you don't have to be an exceptionally powerful person to make things happen; you simply must apply your power over and over, with strategic control, in the same spot. Eventually, all resistance will weaken and conform to the forces you have imposed.

Let's see how this model of the Force is dramatically illustrated in the Star Wars movies, via feats of telekinesis. The most obvious choice is, of course, when a Jedi draws a lightsaber to his hand. It's reminiscent of how a steel object flies across space to snap into the field of a powerful magnet. So let's imagine you're hanging upside down, your feet frozen into a block of ice, in the lair of the monstrous wampa, like Luke in *Episode V: The Empire Strikes Back*. The lightsaber is nearby, but you need it in your hand! We know that the Law of Attraction can only work in concert with the other natural laws. Therefore, barring some paranormal feat, the likes of which have never been scientifically documented, you are not going to be able to instantly get the lightsaber into your hand. However, that doesn't mean you still cannot have that result.

If this scenario were taking place in our reality, you would envision the lightsaber in your hand, over and over again, as strongly and distinctly as possible. Eventually, it would happen. Someone might find you and hand you the lightsaber. Or the ice might crack around your feet, freeing you so you could get to the lightsaber. Or, to be even more extreme, some freakish weather anomaly might break the ice that forms the roof of the cave, bringing you and the lightsaber together.

Would any of these things happen quickly enough to keep you from being devoured by the wampa? Probably not. If I were in that scenario, I would probably forget the lightsaber and instead focus on surviving the ordeal in one piece. After all, that is the actual goal. Getting the lightsaber is a tactic in not being victimized by the monster. See the method of logical thinking here?

There are a number of things that could prevent you from becoming a wampa snack. Maybe he is just not hungry. Maybe a chunk of ice will fall on his head and kill him. Maybe he'll have a heart attack. Or maybe he'll just have a change of heart, because it happens to be a special holiday to him, and he lets you go, just as the U.S. president pardons a Thanksgiving turkey. The point of this is to start thinking differently about your options and to focus on the goal of *what* you want. You shouldn't be invested in exactly *how* that outcome might occur.

Be Aware

The second big issue that determines how long it takes for your wish to come true is *how aware you are of inspiration and opportunities.* Just as you thought of different ways to attract a lightsaber, you must be astute and creative enough to realize when a path to your fulfilled wish has opened right in front of you but by means you did not expect. This is particularly important. If you are wishing for something, there is a good chance you have never had it before. Therefore, when it does begin to materialize, you may not recognize it at first. It may look different than you expected.

I started publishing books when I was a teenager. In my early days as a writer, I wanted to be published by a big national company (of course), but those places would only take submissions through elite agencies. As a kid from the mountains of western North Carolina, I didn't have any contacts with a good agent. I decided to manifest an agent, and started submitting samples of my work to agencies in New York. I received rejection after rejection, but I kept faith in my goal: I would get a big agent who would get me a big publishing deal. One of the rejections included a personal note, saying the agent was sorry, but she always enjoyed visiting Asheville and staying at a particular hotel. Two days later, I got a call from that hotel, asking me if I would give some walking tours for the Halloween season, due to my reputation for telling ghost stories. I found it interesting that this hotel popped up in conjunction with my wish, and my antennae raised.

I did a tour for the hotel, and at the end of it a woman said she would like to learn how to investigate ghosts properly. I went home and wrote a little booklet called *How to Hunt Ghosts*, and printed it on my home computer to sell on my tours. The next time I gave a tour, it was attended by a *New York Times* bestselling author. I gave him a copy of my new booklet, and he invited me and my girl-friend to his house. We became fast friends, and he introduced me, via phone, to his agent in New York. The agent asked me to send a box full of my writing samples. I threw in a variety of stuff and, almost as an afterthought, tossed in a copy of my booklet on ghost hunting. Two weeks later the agent called me and said an editor at a major publishing company loved my booklet. One week later I had my first book deal with a major publisher for a book called—you guessed it—*How to Hunt Ghosts*. That book is now published in numerous languages and read by people around the world.

In this instance things did not evolve just as I expected. I reached my ultimate goal, but I could never have imagined exactly how this whole scenario would unfold. However, I paid attention to the synchronicity when the hotel name popped up in conjunction with my correspondence. When that led me to the woman who wanted a particular product, I paid attention and was inspired to *produce* that product. That was the book that got me the deal I wanted and finally realized my manifestation. As you can see, this is all about looking for clues that lead you in the right direction and then taking action on inspiration. Don't be so foolish that when the opportunities you've created start to open doors right in front of you, you don't go through them. Avoid distractions, and don't be stubborn about how your wish is "supposed" to manifest, or unable to grasp the significance of those moments when the universe unexpectedly talks to you.

Inspiration is a big key here. Sometimes when you put forth a wish the Force rumbles and sends a signal back informing you that all is moving in the right direction, but more action is required by you. You should be just as grateful for those messages as you are when a door swings wide open for you. In fact, you are wise to send forth your intention and wait for the universe to send back the proper instructions to you. This is much more effective than plowing ahead like a bull in a china shop, smashing everything around you because you don't fully understand exactly where your energies should be directed.

Relax, Then Seize

Have you ever struggled trying to swipe a gnat from your drink? Whenever you poke your finger toward it, the gnat always seems to move away. But if you hold your finger still, and wait for a moment, it will probably move closer to you, allowing you to gently swipe it to the side of the cup. Imagine yourself alone in a large swimming pool full of floating inflated beach balls. If you flail around chaotically, you are apt to continually push them away from you. But if you are still, calm, and relaxed, they will float right up to you. In fact, they may even stick to you. You should think of your state during the period of manifestation in a similar way. Instead of bolting after your vision, sit back, calm and relaxed, allowing the things you want to drift toward you. Then, when the timing is right, seize them.

It is important to trust that your intention, projected properly into the universe, is working for you, all the time, in the background, attracting your wishes. Using the Law of Attraction is not just about pushing your demands into the Force, but also being patient enough to receive the fruits of your thoughts in due time. Determining the reasonable timeline within which your intention should materialize reminds us of Obi-Wan's words to Luke as the student trains with the Force on the *Millennium Falcon*. "Let go your conscious self, and act on instinct," the masterful Obi-Wan instructs.

Trust Your Instincts

Acting on instinct may seem like such vague guidance that you find it useless. But the fact is that you do have instincts. Every time you blink your eyes, an instinct is in control. The problem is that in these days of high technology we are more inclined to think like computers, awaiting commands before we act. However, you have an innate sense of whether or not something is working out for you. Sometimes you might feel like walking into a casino and gambling, even though you know statistically the odds are against you. Whether or not you win or lose, the fact you felt inclined to take a chance is based on some instinctual feeling that you *might* win that day. The more you practice your instincts, from a trial and error perspective, the better you will get to know the feelings inside yourself.

Your entire body is so much in sync with the universe that it acts like a binary vessel—contracting when things feel tense and relaxing when things feel good and peaceful. There is an entire field devoted to the study of this called *kinesiology*. These kinds of reactions can even be observed in the most basic life forms. I once wrote a rhyming illustrated children's book called *The Lonely Ameba* (yes, "amoeba" can be spelled without the "o"). It included colorful characters like "Larry the Hairy Paramecium" and "Gene Euglena." But as I did research for this playful, microscopic landscape, I realized something interesting about amoebas. They are just organic sacks without brains or nervous systems. Nonetheless, they are extremely reactive. They tense up and move away from water with an incompatible temperature or salinity. They relax, expand, and thrive, even actively hunt prey. Though our bodies are much more complex than those of amoebas, the same principles apply to our automatic reactions. We also tense up or relax immediately when faced with a particular scenario. It is this innate, subcionsous awareness of our surroundings that most quickly taps into what is "right" or "wrong." This is why, throughout the Star Wars series, Jedis are asked to search their *feelings* more than their minds.

You must stay in tune with the world around you at all times. The information you can glean from your eyes, ears, nose, mouth, and skin is limited. However, you possess this primordial sense called "instinct," which goes back to the very earliest forms of life. The more you can tap into that sense, the more quickly you will be able to manipulate the Force. After all, it is the fundamental part of being alive.

Understand that time is necessary for your seeds to take root, grow, and then eventually pop above the surface. However, if you have drifted away from your manifestation, especially because you feel it is no longer effective, start over again. Revisit your wish anew, given the new conditions in which you find yourself, and start molding it again. Every time you do so, the part of you that can materialize grows and matures more in wisdom.

Physicists and mathematicians understand the three dimensions of the physical universe: up and down, left and right, and front and back. But the fourth dimension, *time*, is still full of mystery. One thing we do know is that a particular point, on its own, may have limited potency. But when that physical point is stretched and dances through time, it gradually takes on a form. For example, a physical point such as your body existed five minutes ago, as well as right now. The relationship between those two points is expressed in time, how one point morphs into another, in the form of a wave. That's why a pulsing energy, low at one moment, then high at the next, can create a sine-wave pattern when extended. The thought you wish to manifest starts as a particular impression upon a particular point, but over time you must constantly control the shape it takes by managing its flow—determining its ultimate form. The amount of time needed to do this depends on the magnitude and complexity of the structure you intend to create. Take all of this into consideration as you feel how long it should take for your wish to manifest. Donald Trump can probably manifest $1 million more quickly than you, given his overall relationship to the goal. But there are many things you can manifest more quickly than him. Once you know what you want, take a realistic look at your relationship to the variables, then feel the appropriate timeline from there.

Regardless of what you might manifest, there is one looming monster that will quickly take you down if you're not eternally vigilant. Always, always, always, avoid the negative. This leads us to the next big consideration along your journey with the Force.

Chapter Seven

Avoid the Negative

"There's no mystical energy field
[that] controls *my* destiny."

—Han Solo, *Episode IV: A New Hope*

Early in this process, as you prepared yourself to start manifesting, you began reformatting your brain. A big part of that was: *Stay away from things that make you feel bad.* However, as time passes, you have no doubt seen that this is much easier said than done. Most of the people you probably know have a cynical and pessimistic view of the world. This is not surprising, given the normal aspects of upbringing we have already covered. Additionally, the happier and more positive you become, the more you will stand out in contrast to them, making them even more agitated and envious of your newfound optimism. Even good friends may arrogantly dismiss the attitude you are embracing. Surely you've heard the phrase *misery loves company.* Many people who cling to the comfort of a disappointing life do not want to see someone else obtain happiness. Unfortunately, even good people sometimes give up on life. They choose to expect disappointment so that they will not be disappointed. This puts them in a downward spiral, perpetually attracting more disappointing things into their lives.

To get away from all the negative comments and thoughts around you, you might feel as if you want to hole yourself up in a cave somewhere! Fortunately, that is not always necessary. While you are in the process of learning to use the Force, it is true that you should spend a minimum amount of time around negative people, even family and friends. But later, after you've become a Jedi, you will be strong enough to go back and act as a mentor if you want, teaching them what you have learned and giving them real-world examples of your success. You can help them tremendously. In the meantime, as you develop, when you know you have to be around someone who will pull down your spirit, or if something unexpectedly happens that fills you with a sense of darkness, here is the technique for handling it: *Draw on a positive memory bank.*

Your Positive Life

One of the most enjoyable aspects of learning to use the Force is creating your very own file of positive, joyous memories. Most of the power of the Force comes from your mind, so when your mind is filled with good, vivid thoughts, you will have no choice but to continue projecting that energy, and therefore receiving the positive back in your direction. When it comes to controlling your mind, pretending and play-acting are just as powerful as the real thing. Sit down with a pen and paper and make a list of the five happiest moments of your life.

When you make this list, you have to be completely honest with yourself. It can be as simple as "watching the sun set over my backyard," "playing with my new puppy," or "eating strawberry cake." Or you can use more detail, like "hearing the applause from my coworkers when I received my gift at the 2007 Christmas party in Aspen." You can even be graphic, if you want to relive a special, intimate moment with your partner. The most important thing about each item on the list is that you can recall it quickly and vividly, and it instantly makes you feel good.

Once you have decided on the five things, keep the list to yourself. Sit down, mull it over, and remember the one thing that makes you feel the *best* over and over again until it is thoroughly burned into your mind. That memory will be your instant "go-to" memory whenever someone, or something, says or does something that starts to make you feel negative. Therefore, it is of the utmost importance. This will not only affect you mentally, but will have an impact physically, as well.

I remember one night in 2007, when I was sitting with a group of friends on a blue, slag-stone street in Old San Juan, Puerto Rico.

Distant salsa music was bumping in the warm air as I sipped on an ice-cold mojito. I looked down the street, and the orange, incandescent lights from a row of bars and restaurants glinted off the 500-year-old stone architecture. The shadows wavered slightly as a tropical ocean breeze gently passed through. It felt perfect on the flesh. At that moment I realized that I had never been happier.

Later that night, a couple of buddies and I were horsing around in a cruise ship swimming pool. Eventually, our challenges led to a breath-holding contest, and I learned something truly remarkable. Once fully submerged, I could hold my breath *much* longer—perhaps even twice as long—if I immediately switched my thoughts back to that positive memory on the San Juan street. No one could beat me. By putting myself into that positive state, due to my vivid mental recall, my entire body physically calmed so much that I needed less air to survive. This means that the more you learn to keep your mind in a good place, the happier and *longer* your life can be!

Once you have chosen your top positive memory, use it to combat any external force that may try to drag you down to a lower, less-confident state of mind. You should train yourself to snap to it in an instant, and hold it in your mind as long, and as often, as needed to keep the gloomy energies at bay until they dissipate. It can be difficult for you to quickly realize that you are being subjected to adverse input. By now, you've unfortunately lived long enough to expect unfavorable talk, so it may take a while for you to grasp when it's happening around you or to you.

Knowing You're Calm

As Luke trains on Dagobah, toting Yoda around on his back, he pauses to ask the Jedi master a question about discernment: "How am I to know the good side [of the Force] from the bad?"

"You will know. When you're calm, at peace. Passive," Yoda assures him.

As soon as you notice that you are starting to feel pessimistic, snap to your positive memory bank and use it to calm yourself and keep your smile. As time goes on, you may find that you have used your top positive memory so many times that it has begun to lose its full power. In that case, re-examine your list of five, and pick another thing that gives you this strong sense. What's even better is that once you've started down this new road of using the Law of Attraction, so many good things will begin pouring into your life that you'll constantly have to revise your list. But definitely be sure to always have one predetermined memory you will use to hold your mental ground whenever you feel you are slipping.

Negative or Lack of Positive?

There is another good question that arises as we try to figure out the best way to ensure we take the right path: Is the negative the same thing as the *lack of positive*? Life is so full of complicated issues that we humans are not smart enough to determine all outcomes and choices. For example, "You are either with me or against me" is a very immature and foolishly oversimplified phrase. Fortunately for us, the process of using the Force is not about reaching a philosophical understanding of all the world's problems. It is only about understanding the way your mind will work and doing all you can to make sure you are projecting, and therefore receiving, the most helpful energy possible. So, for our purposes, when we ask if lack of positive equals negative, the answer is "yes." Because the tendency of the world is to be negative, you must overcompensate by filling your mind only with the positive. You cannot allow your work to be sidetracked, and to diffuse your entire operation.

The Mindful Mind

A huge leap forward in understanding how to use the Force is based on your ability to take responsibility for yourself and your own thinking. The primitive side of us is inclined to envision ourselves as beings who are reacting to the external situations around us. However, using the Force is to feel the exact opposite; you are, in fact, in control at all times, and no one truly has the power to sway you from your self-chosen destiny. You must not be *reactive*, but *proactive*.

If someone says something nasty to you, your instinct will be to scramble and attack back at them. However, this may not always be the best course of action. If you do that, you are allowing that other person to set the stage and control the entire scenario. You cannot affect how another person acts or behaves, but you can manage yourself. So stay focused on where your personal power truly lies—in your ability to manage yourself. If you remember that *energy flows where attention goes*, you can, in fact, manipulate the situation by not responding to the things that put you on the defensive. Instead, put your power behind the positive statements that allow you to hold your ground, or to go on the offensive yourself, if need be.

Dr. Hew Len, practitioner of the Hawaiian self-help system known as Ho'oponopono, is credited with the observation, "Ever notice that when there's a problem, *you're* there?" His point is quite straightforward. Every time you encounter what you feel is an obstacle, the best way to scientifically dissect it is to look at all the components present. Obviously, since you are present, you are one of the components.

This stage of avoiding the negative requires you to examine yourself and consider as best you can what energy you're contributing to the scenario. Time and time again, people have aggressively tried to drag me into arguments about spiritual topics. Because of my work with ghosts, a typical challenge might be, "Since the *Bible* says your spirit goes to God when you die, how is it possible for ghosts to exist?" I am quick to point out that there are ghosts of all kinds of things, including inanimate objects. People see ghost ships, ghost airplanes, and ghost stagecoaches, as well as the horses pulling them. It is a mistake to think that ghosts are simply part of the human spirit. In doing so, I change the entire premise of the question to a better-informed and more accurate one, and this shifts the energy into a new direction, favorable to me and my knowledge.

It is also interesting to think about another aspect of the Star Wars movies, called the *Force ghost*. Throughout the films, the ghosts of Obi-Wan, Yoda, and even Anakin appear after death. They each show up clothed, and since clothing is an inanimate object, it makes us further question the nature of their manifestations. Maybe, once again, these are not remnants that have returned from some spiritual realm, but projections from the minds of the living. They could be spirits of the dead, or some form or hallucination, or a combination of both—we are never explicitly told in the films. The point is that what resides inside your own head determines the reality that you ultimately experience, even if it seems to be outside yourself. Luke sees the ghost of his mentor Obi-Wan because he *needs* to see it.

You might look at a piece of chocolate cake and imagine that it possesses qualities that you will enjoy when you take it into your mouth. However, what you experience when you eat that cake is yours alone. You cannot scientifically prove to another person what you perceive when you bite into the cake. It may be something that is pleasurable to you, but you have no way of sharing that exact experience with another, though you both call it pleasurable. There is a point where the so-called outside world interfaces with the inside world to produce your experience, and yet, in the long run, all that is actually real to you is your own perception.

The Dangers of Solipsism

Because we expect the external world to directly relate to our internal worlds, we can be easily fooled. Scientists, magicians, and marketers delight in taking our expectations of the "outside world" and using them to trick us. This, however, does not mean we should see the world in what philosophers call a "solipsistic" way.

Solipsism comes from the Latin words *solus*, meaning "alone," and *ipse*, meaning "self." It is the idea that only one's own mind is sure to exist; the external world and other minds cannot be known by any means other than your perception of them. It's even possible they have no reality outside your own mind. In other words, *you* are the only thing that exists, and the entire world you think is real exists only in your mind, no different from a realistic dream. This kind of concept has been exploited in movies like *The Matrix*, in which much of your perceived reality is actually a simulated reality.

To be absolutely honest, there is no way of disproving solipsism. It may be that I, Joshua P. Warren, am the only person in the world, and I am writing this book for myself, though I believe in the illusion that it will be read by others. You can say that yours is the only mind that exists, and you, for whatever reason, attracted this book and the concept of my being into your life. From a scientific point of view, there is no way of disproving these scenarios. Fortunately, once again, the purpose of this book is not to reach a philosophical understanding of all the world's great mysteries. It is only about accepting the way your mind will work. It is a practical guide, and we are doing all we can to make sure you are transmitting, and therefore receiving, the most helpful energy possible. To that end, what you must do is forget about all the things you cannot know, and focus on the things you must do in order to shape your experience through the Force.

Imagine yourself as a co-creator of what comes next; be it the next moment, minute, hour, day, week, month, or year. You must use your instincts to feel the balance somewhere between solipsism—thinking you control everything—and victimization— thinking you control nothing. That balance is the realm in which you become the co-creator of what will happen next.

Extremes are always bad. Solipsism can lead to megalomania, but a victimization mindset is just as bad, and will always lead to the dark side. One of the biggest pitfalls that will threaten you, and your evolution to success, is the victim mindset. Even if you have been a victim in the past, continuing to feel like you are one will only attract more things that make you feel like a victim.

Say No to Victimhood

It is just as important to avoid the negative feelings in yourself as it is to resist those that come from others. In fact, for many, it is actually easier to stay away from the bad input of friends or family than it is to avoid the dark things that haunt us inside, wherever we go and whatever we do. Remember that in order to project good energy you need to attract more good energy. You must forgive everyone, including yourself. Though you may have been a victim in the past, you must accept that you are not a victim *now*. Furthermore, you will not ever be one again. All must feel good and compassionate inside you.

If you have hatred toward someone, or you fear another, you must stop feeling that way. Pay attention to where you are *right this moment*, and do not allow those feelings of anger or fear to swell up inside you. Whenever you feel it happening, strongly switch your thoughts to the memory bank of good experiences, and allow only those visions to place an aura of protection around you.

In *Episode II: Attack of the Clones*, padawan Anakin is worried about his relationship with Padmé. "She's forgotten me completely," he says.

His master, Obi-Wan, is quick to remind Anakin he is allowing his thoughts to slip unhealthily. "You're focusing on the negative, Anakin. Be mindful of your thoughts."

As you continue the process of successfully using the Force, let this be the keystone of your philosophy every moment of every day.

Chapter Eight

Daily Reminders

"Keep your concentration here and now,
where it belongs."

—Qui-Gon Jinn, *Episode I: The Phantom Menace*

As an American, I grew up laughing at skits on *Saturday Night Live*. When it comes to daily affirmations, it's hard to forget the silly character of Stuart Smalley, played by Al Franken (who surprised everyone by later becoming a U.S. Senator in real life). He satirized sensitive self-help gurus, and popularized the affirmation, "I'm good enough, I'm smart enough, and doggone it, people like me!" Though easy fodder for a comedy skit, there is no doubt that daily affirmations play an extremely powerful role in helping you to stay on track, keeping your visualizations clear and consistent, day after day. However, you must fully understand why and how to use them, or you could accidentally work against your wishes.

The purpose of daily reminders is quite self-explanatory. When you wake up each day, you may find yourself in a rush, especially if you've hit the snooze button a few too many times. In the blur of activity that starts your day, it is easy to forget about the thing you want to manifest. However, it is extremely important that you take the previous day and string it to the current one. Sleep time is when your brain reboots and your body repairs itself, but it is not meant to weaken or wipe clean your long-term goal. In fact, each time you sleep, rest should strengthen your overall plan and resolve.

To make matters worse, most of us tune into some kind of media when we start the day. This is partly necessary in order to check the weather, traffic, or other conditions that might influence how we proceed. However, those messages are always brought to you at a cost: sponsors. As you know, sponsors are trying to sell you something, in one way or another. A seller's livelihood is based on convincing you that you need something. Therefore you will hear lots of messages that imply, in some way, that you are lacking something in your life. They seek to sap your self confidence, suggesting you are in a lower class than you should be. Companies spend millions of dollars every day on psychologists who do extensive scientific research to learn the most effective way to influence your behavior. They have narrowed it down to whether or not you will walk into a store, then whether you will turn right or left, or look up or down. We are all rats in a giant capitalistic lab; you must combat this by *producing your own customized, personalized, positive ad campaign, targeted only at yourself.*

Effective Affirmations

It is relatively easy to feed valuable commands into your subconsious mind that will automatically improve your life. However, they will only work properly if you adhere to a few basic tips that are often overlooked.

Find a Good Spot

What are the physical areas and objects around you to which you pay the most attention each day? Is it the ceiling when you're lying in bed? Is it the display on your cell phone? Your mirror in the bathroom? Your refrigerator? Your car radio? Even if every day is different for you, find the areas that you will probably look at on a daily basis. These are the prime locations for your reminders, real estate for your own tiny billboards. In each one of these locations, stick a paper note that will prompt you to mentally broadcast your goal once again. Finding the best places to put your notes isn't a problem. Wording them correctly is what takes more skill.

Keep It Positive and Honest

Always word your reminders in the positive, and usually in the active, present tense. For example, instead of writing "I will not gain weight," write "I am in the process of slimming." Or instead of writing "I will not be poor," write "I am attracting great wealth." This concept goes back to our mental exercise regarding Luke in the wampa's cave. Instead of thinking "I will not be eaten by the wampa," it would be more effective to think "I will survive the wampa in one healthy piece." All this is based on that fortunate fact that a positive thought is stronger than a negative thought. It is extremely easy to forget this, so you must be especially mindful of this when forming your affirmations.

The reminders must always feel honest to you. This one is so crucial and misunderstood that it alone ruins more affirmations than anything else. For example, if I want to lose weight, it might seem natural for me to write an affirmation saying "I am slim." However, in reality, if you are not slim and you read this, it will digress so much from your present condition that it will remind you how *far* away you are from your goal. That means it will, in practice, actually make you feel fatter; that feeling, projected into the universe, will actually *make* you fatter, thereby achieving the opposite result. If you have pennies in your pocket and read an affirmation saying "I am rich," once again, this will state such a blatant untruth that its backlash will drive you into a greater feeling of poverty. As you can see, there is a much more to producing effective affirmations than you might think. It goes miles beyond "I'm good enough, I'm smart enough, and doggone it, people like me!"

When formulating successful daily reminders, you have to sit back and judge how what you write makes you feel both consciously and subconsciously. What flashes in your mind? It *must, must, must* be a good thing for the affirmation to work the way you intend. It is always good to start with the words "I am," but after those words is where things get tricky. Some people are able to say "I am driving my new car," and it works. Those words, in that order, make them feel good enough to send the powerful signals to manifest things. However, in my own life, I might choose to say "I am attracting my new car" instead. I have a very logical and scientific mind. Consequently, if I state something that is not presently true, it usually makes me feel dishonest. However, if I can word it in a way that indicates the active, kinetic work in progress, this feels better. Hence, the signals I send out are more pure and real to me.

Jedis often use the power of affirmations to promote lessons. During his training, when Luke says to Yoda, "I am not afraid," Yoda stresses his own affirmation. "You *will* be," he replies. This is a troubling moment, as we understand that Yoda is weakening Luke's affirmation, forcing Luke to face his fears in advance of physical combat.

You have to play around with your affirmations. Do you prefer using phrases like "I am in the process of attracting," "I am days away from," "I am manifesting," or just "I am"? You must figure this out for yourself. You may spend days working on the one, perfect reminder for your particular project. That is fine. These notes are important, so you should take the necessary amount of time to get them just right. There are other considerations that can also help make them as impressive as possible.

Include Details

Just as your visions should be detailed, your reminders will benefit from being detailed as well. Again, however, if you are too wordy, the note loses its impact; if you are not detailed enough, it might not capture the feeling you want as accurately as it could. So you should think about each of the five senses related to your affirmation and pick one or two that might help really bring it to life. Instead of writing "I am attracting my house by the beach," I might write "I am attracting my blue house by the warm, sunny beach." Or, instead of writing "I am attracting my own restaurant," I might write "I am attracting my own restaurant that smells like Grandma's kitchen." Keep in mind that the right side of the brain, the part that deals with imagination, is the section that gives power to your visualizations. This area is stimulated by sensory input, and the more your affirmations connect with your subjective humanity, the better.

Highly advanced computers such as C-3PO may appear and behave like human beings (C-3PO even has some element in his programming that makes him an odd combination of cowardly and pessimistic: "We're doomed!" he moans on more than one occasion). However, they are distinctly inhuman. Organic cells are able to naturally reproduce and transfer energy from one organism into another over generations. C-3PO's metal body cannot do this. The tradeoff is that it's much easier to bring him back to life, since his metal body is much more durable. He can be (and is) ripped apart and reassembled over and over again. The point here is that it is not the part of your brain that is wired like C-3PO's that gives the energy to your manifestation. It is that other part of the brain, most connected to bearing organic offspring, which gives the same kind of energy to your mental offspring. Always appeal to that emotional side of yourself instead of thinking like a computer.

Public or Private?

The reminders you leave should also be extremely personal. This can cause a whole new set of problems for some people. Unless you live alone, someone else is likely to see what you've posted on the refrigerator or bathroom mirror. By allowing someone else to see your affirmations, you're taking a risk that he or she may not be on board with your thoughts, and might make some critical statement. This embarrassment can do deep damage to your progress. There are a couple of ways to handle this.

You should always be very particular about where you post your reminders. If you share your life with another person who grasps your methods and honestly wants to help you manifest the same things, it is fine for him or her to see your notes. It is especially healthy for married couples, for example, to share identical goals and work together to manifest something. If, however, you feel the wisest route is to keep your operation to yourself, think about the places you are most likely to see and pay attention to your affirmations without exposing them to anyone else. Though this takes some planning and strategy, it is well worth the effort.

You can also post your notes in some kind of coded form. For example, if you want to say "I am attracting a fluffy, white poodle," you might just write the first letter of each word, "I A A A F W P." Even if someone asks you what in the world this gibberish is that you're posting, you can simply say you are doing an experiment with "good luck." Most people are so familiar with superstitions that they will just roll their eyes and blow it off. You, however, will know what it means, and thus the result for you will be the same as if you read the entire written-out sentence.

Mental Associations

I have also found it helpful to create mental associations with things I happen to see every day. If, each day when I leave the house, I drive by a prominent McDonald's restaurant and see the iconic golden arches, I might choose to associate those arches with the gateway to my wishes coming true. Maybe turning the ignition to crank up your car reminds you that you are "starting up" your affirmation for the day. Though your reminder is not explicitly spelled out in plain language, your thoughts will kick in and broadcast the vision into the cosmos, stirring the Force to continue working on your behalf. In fact, these kinds of associations can be even more powerful than just looking at words on paper, since they occur in conjunction with an action. Whenever you do something combined with an action, it triggers your brain to feel even more strongly that something real is occurring, changing, and developing.

A big part of using the Force is for you to have a plan behind the obvious plan. I am reminded of the moment in *Episode VI: Return of the Jedi* when Han, Luke, and Leia, inside a spaceship, are trying to slip through an Imperial blockade using a black market entry code. Monitoring the situation, Vader asks an officer, "Where is that shuttle going?" Vader is told the ship was about to be cleared to land on Endor. Vader uses the Force to sense that Luke is on board the incoming ship.

"Shall I hold them?" asks the officer.

"No, leave them to me," Vader replies. "I will deal with them myself."

Vader allows his enemies to pass so he can have them even more tightly in his grasp. Everyone is oblivious to what is happening except for Vader and Luke. Both of them use the Force, sensing each other, and they understand the underlying meaning behind what is happening. You must sometimes conduct yourself like them during this phase of your progress. Those who do not understand will see nothing extraordinary; you, on the other hand, are able to glean the true meaning for your *own* big picture.

A Few More Questions

There are a couple other questions you may have about leaving effective affirmations for yourself:

- *Should I write them in my own hand or print them out on a computer?* You should do whatever feels most authoritative to you, and this depends on your background. There was a time when a letter needed to be handwritten in order to seem heartfelt and honest. If you connect with that approach, take time to carefully write in longhand. I, however, have primarily lived in an age where seeing something printed by a computer printer seems to carry more weight. Because of that, I like to print out my affirmations via computer. I also like the fact that this is a multistep method, taking up even more of my time and therefore stretching out the original thought process. I must first sit down and open a word processing program. Then I must write the affirmation and size it. Next, I must print it out to confirm it is the right size. If so, I have to find a pair of scissors and cut it out. Then I look for tape, apply that tape, and position the affirmation. This takes more effort than simply jotting a few words on a Post-it note and slapping it on a mirror. In my world, my method makes more of a psychological impact.

- *Where should I place reminders?* Place your reminders in spots that you associate with positive feelings. Never underestimate the impact of simple things, such as hot or cold temperatures. If you dread getting into a cold car every day, don't put your note in that place. On the other hand, if you look forward to taking a nice hot shower or bubble bath, consider putting your affirmation on the shampoo bottle. Sure, that means you will have to spend some extra time waterproofing it by putting it in a plastic bag, but that is okay. If there is a cabinet that holds your favorite snacks, that's also a great place to put your words.

Spend time thinking about the things you do each day that you enjoy the most. It seems odd that we must pause and ponder these things. But it just shows how surprisingly out of touch most of us naturally are when it comes to the automated actions of our daily lives. This also bring us to another big consideration in using this method.

Constantly Re-Examine

Humans are creatures of habit who are naturally inclined to process the things we see, and then stop noticing them over time. This can work very much in your favor. If you live in a noisy neighborhood, given enough time, you can tune out the background distractions. I know people who live in towns that stink to high heaven due to factories that pump waste into the air, but these people can't smell the unpleasant aroma. They're around it so much that they've learned to ignore it. This self-defense mechanism of the brain can be helpful. It's what allows you to sit at a table in a crowded restaurant with a number of people all talking at once, but only tune into the conversation that interests you. Though this is generally positive, it is a hindrance to the affirmation process.

With time, the notes you have placed will gradually fade into the background noise of your environment. This is a very bad thing. As your affirmations fade away, so do the visualizations you have attached to them—and remember, the visualizations are ultimately what do all the work here, making your visions manifest in reality. There is nothing you can do to prevent this natural fading from occurring. However, you must try to recognize that it's taken place. If you look directly at one of your notes and your brain struggles to process it, you know it is time to switch up and refresh things.

You can be on the safe side and switch around your affirmations every week, like clockwork. Otherwise, do it when you see they have lost their effectiveness. If you like them, you should keep the same affirmations, but find a new way to place them so that you will notice them prominently once again. The more you do this, the more creative you will become. One of the great things about using the Force is that it constantly forces you to re-examine your own perception of the world around you. You will be surprised by how much more you take in. Your sense of awareness will skyrocket. As time goes on, adjust your affirmations to reflect the progress you are making, honing in, more and more, on your specific goal.

Since the beginning of recorded history, cultures around the world have embraced what we might call "magical thinking." It is the concept that ideas, when represented with words, can help make things occur in the externalized reality. Call them prayers, spells, or even curses (depending on the intention)—taking something from inside your perception and representing it through words, be they spoken or written, is the most basic form of magic. I don't have one universal, magical spell for you, but you will quickly learn why this extremely simple method works so well and has been so highly regarded. With practice, your wishes will become more and more effective, as they bring you more and more in balance with the Force.

Chapter Nine

Perfect Balance

"You refer to the prophecy of the one who
will bring balance to the Force.
You believe it's this boy?"

—Mace Windu, *Episode I: The Phantom Menace*

For thousands of years, mystery schools around the world exploring philosophy, metaphysics and mysticism, have been inspired by Hermetic texts, attributed to a mysterious ancient figure known as Hermes Trismegistus. One of the most influential phrases has been "as above, so below." The full maxim, as translated by Dennis W. Hauck in *The Emerald Tablet: Alchemy for Personal Transformation* is, "That which is Below corresponds to that which is Above, and that which is Above corresponds to that which is Below, to accomplish the miracle of the One Thing."

Unfortunately, humans tend to envision themselves separate from the environment. Many subconsciously fancy themselves quiet audience members watching a great dramatic presentation unfold all around them. Regardless of how huge and complex the universe may be, you are a part of it; all of its wonders exist within you, and conversely, all of your thoughts, feelings, and actions exist within its fabric. Philosopher Alan Watts eloquently said, "Through our eyes, the universe is perceiving itself. Through our ears, the universe is listening to its harmonies. We are the witnesses through which the universe becomes conscious of its glory, of its magnificence." From even the most strict, skeptical, scientific point of view, you are at one with the universe—the very mind that defines its presence. The question is only, how aware are you of this oneness?

A Shift in the Force

Frequently, throughout the Star Wars movies, a Jedi will feel something shift in the overall Force. Perhaps the best example comes in the original film, just after Governor Tarkin uses the Death Star to ruthlessly destroy Princess Leia's home planet, Alderaan. The planet explodes in an instant, and far away, on the *Millennium Falcon*, Obi-Wan suddenly becomes weak-kneed. "Are you all right?" Luke asks. "What's wrong?"

"I felt a great disturbance in the Force," Obi-Wan answers somberly, "as if millions of voices suddenly cried out in terror and were suddenly silenced. I feel something terrible has happened."

It is absolutely true that as your exercises proceed and you become even more aware of your environment, your sensitivity to the balance around you will also increase. In fact, there will be days when, no matter how clear and positive your visions and intentions may be, it seems the entire Force is simply in a rocky state. Remember that you live in concert with the universe, but that does not mean you control it. There will be days when you wake up and everything seems to go wrong, one incident after another. However, it is at those times that it is most important for you to use the Force, doing your best to readjust things around you, bending them back to the positive world you want to experience. This brings us to an extremely important point in the process: *As you change the world, some things must break down so that others can be born.*

Throughout your entire life you've heard conventional wisdom, like "Every cloud has a silver lining," or, as Helen Keller and many others have said, "When one door closes, another opens." Up until now, you may have felt these kinds of sentiments were just condolences, a last attempt to cheer up someone in hopeless circumstances. However, you now must understand completely that these phrases are true. You cannot move forward in your life and also stay in the same position. Change is required.

Everything in the universe exists in a state of balance. If nothing else, the scientific method has confirmed this again and again. Each time we have been able to examine, test, and experiment with a closed, controlled system, we see the marvelous symmetry as energy transforms from one state to another but always remains present. This is stated in the Law of Conservation of Energy, that *energy can be neither created nor destroyed, but it can change form.*

The purpose of using the Force is to affect the world around you. That means you are producing change in your personal system, or set of experiences. When your wish begins to take hold and rearrange the world to suit your fancy, energy will be removed from some places and transferred to others. That means you must expect to see some things break down and disappear in order for the new circumstances to evolve. It is important that you keep a clear head and do not panic as this happens. Humans are used to experiencing change—it will occur, in some form, whether you like it or not—throughout life. But when you use the Force that rate of change is accelerated, and things will happen according to the intense directives you have transmitted, as opposed to some more diffuse mix of intentions, which is what generally happens around most untrained people.

Some reading this book may have only now realized what I have just described. The true power inside you may suddenly be intimidating. You may feel, "I am not wise enough to make the right changes in my life. I am not informed enough to know what's best for me. What if I screw up? I don't want this power, after all!" Well, don't worry about that. The underlying message of this material is that you are already manifesting what you want every moment of every day, whether you like it or not. You have no choice. And so you may as well start at least becoming more aware of the situation so you can keep things positive.

Love Brings Success

Here is something that should comfort you: *If you sincerely project positive, loving, happy wishes, then it is impossible for any of those wishes to have a bad outcome.* Even if something must break down or rearrange itself in order for your manifestation to occur, it was for the best, as decided by the eternal balance of the universe. Just as you did not create this world, you cannot take responsibility for how things function here. This does not contradict the idea that you and the universe are one. That's because you and the universe are *now* one. Who knows what happened before you were born?

Failure Leads to Success

Throughout my life, each time something seemed like an immediate failure, it actually opened the door for something much better. I was once shocked when what I thought was the perfect publisher for a book turned it down. Thank goodness that happened, because it ended up being published by a much larger, more esteemed company. I made a lot more money and it reached more people. The first time I pitched my radio show, *Speaking of Strange*, it was turned down by a little station. Thank goodness that happened, since I would have been locked in a contract, and a much bigger, better station eventually chose to air it. And sometimes we should be very grateful that certain things fail altogether, since they might brand us for life if they succeeded! Every time a relationship has ended, be it personal or professional, I feel it cleared the way for a better person to appear. Perhaps you've heard the old adage, "When the student is ready, the master shall appear." We are all students, and each person who appears is a potential master, there to teach us something we need to know about life at that particular time.

___

Fear Is Not an Option

The best way to make sure you are always projecting the right vibes into the Force is to never, *ever* act out of fear (of any kind). When you are afraid, you are mentally screaming, "I am weak!" When you transmit weakness, then not only do you become weaker, but more and more predators will be attracted to you. This is no different than how it works in the animal world.

I was once interviewed on the Animal Planet channel about strange pets. A story had surfaced about a cat named Oscar at a nursing home in Providence, Rhode Island. Oscar had gained fame, if not infamy, for being able to predict when someone was about to die. He would make the rounds each day, sniffing at patients. When he curled up with certain ones, they would usually die within a few hours. As of this writing, the medical professionals say he has correctly predicted the deaths of more than fifty people. The TV show producers asked me to give my opinion of how this was possible.

I answered that this kind of thing is not unusual at all in the animal kingdom. In fact, scientists are still unsure about how flies appear so quickly on dead bodies. Often they travel from many miles away, farther than the stench of death should have drifted in such a short period of time. When it comes to cats and dogs in particular, because we have domesticated them and love them for their cuddliness and companionship, it is easy to forget that they have evolved as predators over millions of years. In order to survive, they must be able to sense weakness. In the wild, in order to stay alive, you want to get food with as little effort as possible. It makes sense that these predators can pick up on some projection into the Force that death is imminent, and the prey is "easy pickings." It may not be something we can currently explain scientifically, but it must be a crucial element in how life has sustained itself here for so long. Humans, too, are predators. If you think weak thoughts, or project fear into the Force, someone or something will notice since we are all interconnected. The result can never be good for you.

You, and the Collective

When using the Force to produce results for yourself, *you can make the most of your efforts by considering your relationship to the entire universe, including all the people within.* Though your intentions may be strong, they are not the only intentions at play in the world. One simple example of this, to which many can relate, is the process of gambling.

Gambling is a good model for human intentions since when money is on the line, people become exceptionally focused. I used to produce big paranormal conferences at the Grove Park Inn in Asheville, North Carolina. One of my favorite sessions was what I called "Psychic Games." I would stand in front of a crowd of hundreds and pull a single card from a deck of symbols. Then I would ask everyone to stand. Next, I would say, "If you think this card has a circle on it, sit down." A good section of the people would. Next, I might say, "If you think this card has a triangle on it, sit down." This would continue until I had a small section of the audience standing, and I would invite those folks up to be the players.

Once onstage, I would give the contestants a series of challenges. One might be to telepathically project a number to another person. Or I might roll a die and ask the person to control the number facing upward. In the first round, everyone had fun and half-heartedly participated. But when round two came, I pulled a wad of cash from my pocket and said, "Things will change a bit now. From here on out, whenever you win a round I will give you a fresh, crisp $20 bill." I could immediately see the players sit up, open their eyes more, quiet down, and pay much more attention.

From that point on, though we played the exact same games over and over, I found that the same person or two would win time and time again. Why? Because I had now introduced a reward that connected with their survival instinct, and those were the people who were *truly* the most in touch with their "sixth sense." If a sixth sense exists, it is for the same reason the other five senses evolved: to assist in human survival. There was a time when that skill would have been focused on hunting an animal or understanding the seasons to enhance the harvest. In fact, a caveman would have had little interest in my $20 bill. But here in America, we now live in an age in which money equals survival; developing an instinct for obtaining money, then, is an evolutionary advantage.

I give you this example because it makes it easier to understand your personal world in relation to society, regarding survival and money. If you choose to use the Force to outright gamble for money, be aware of how your intentions compare to the resistance. If you decide to play a typical lottery, then your intention is up against the intentions of *every* other person who has bought the same ticket. You are all mentally competing for the same thing. As you may recall, I have warned against that mentality. That means if you expect yourself to be the winner, then you had better really think highly of your skills to powerhouse your intent above all others in the lottery. In many cases, no one wins because the overall mix is so cluttered that each use of the Force cancels out the others.

From this point of view, you are actually much more apt to find success if you simply walk into a casino to gamble. Those who have designed and operate the games already have the advantage, of course, but at least all the intentions involved are spread over more surface area. This means your intention can have an even bigger impact on any one site at any one time than if you are part of a stampede of people all clamoring for the same thing. I give this only as an example of how collective humanity works in real life. I do not condone gambling unless it is done for fun alone. But, let's face it, all of life is a form of gambling. So you are actually much better off staying out of the gambling establishments that have perfected the art of reducing your chances. Instead, focus that energy on other elements in life where less competition exists. This is why being aware of inspiration is so important—allowing you to notice areas in your life where opportunity lies, where there are a much more limited number of people clawing for the same thing at the same time.

A Symbiotic Relationship

In *Episode I: The Phantom Menace*, as Qui-Gon Jinn and a young Obi-Wan stand before Boss Nass, head of the Gungans, they discuss the impact of a droid army on the verge of attacking the Naboo, the enemies of the Gungans. Boss Nass does not care if Naboo is about to be invaded, stating that the society of his native species will remain secure. Obi-Wan tells him, "You and the Naboo form a symbiont circle. What happens to one of you will affect the other. You must understand this."

It is fitting for the entire Star Wars saga that this statement should come early on in *Episode I*. This exemplifies the significance of the Force. As the saying goes, "No man is an island," and you would be foolish to remove yourself from those around you. If your neighbor's house is burning down, you could coldly dismiss his plight, thankful that it is not your own. However, if that fire is allowed to continue burning, it will spread and may well burn down your house in the long run. If sick people come into your community and are not treated, then that sickness may spread to you and your loved ones. Unfortunately, humanitarian causes and assisting one's fellow humans have often been viewed as unimportant. But the hard fact is that what happens to another person can happen to you.

When you realize that we all are energies swirling to attain balance in the same system, you will feel the Force strongly not only in yourself, but in all those around you. This is how and when your awareness will expand beyond yourself, and to the collective. Scientists tell us there is a biological Adam and Eve, individuals from whom the physical genes in your body, and the body of every living human, descended. That means we are all part of the same giant organism. People around the globe have their own traditions and experiences, yet our commonalities far outweigh our differences.

You should not only be willing to look out for others as best you can, but also to ask for help when you feel you need it. Asking for help is not a sign of weakness. It is an acknowledgement that another person is in balance with you and can provide you with something you currently lack. You should, however, be able to provide something in return, retaining that reciprocal symmetry. It is not right to ask without giving, though, and remember that you must give to receive. Many people actually enjoy being asked for help. It reinforces their own sense of self-worth, proving they have attained the ability to provide for others in need.

"You're My Only Hope"

Among the most famous scenes in *Episode IV: A New Hope* is the moment when Princess Leia, her ship having been boarded by Imperial forces, inserts something into R2-D2 containing a message for Obi-Wan, asking for his help. One can understand her irritation when her message is answered not by the famous general, but by a farm boy from Tatooine and his mercenary companion.

Whether we want the responsibility or not, it is up to us to be the custodians of the whole. From a physical perspective alone, our planet Earth is a bubble of life in the midst of a vast galaxy of harsh, lifeless planets. The life that our planet sustains is precious and fragile. If you smoke a cigarette in a hotel room, that smoke lingers the rest of the night, irritating your breathing. When it finally settles, it is a black film on everything, and each subsequent cigarette layers on more and more. Eventually a housekeeper must come in, wipe away all the residue, and throw the black rags somewhere else. But what happens when there is no other place to throw the waste? We must live with the consequences of our actions for a long time.

Chapter Ten

The Mirror Effect

"Why, you stuck-up, half-witted,
scruffy-looking nerf herder!"

—Princess Leia to Han Solo, *Episode V: The Empire Strikes Back*

Once you start to see practical results and realize that you can indeed manifest things in the world around you by using the Force, an even deeper level of self-understanding is necessary. The first thing to comprehend is that, in order to truly appreciate and wisely alter your reality, you must fully grasp your own identity and ego. This entails what is known as the "mirror effect."

Let us imagine you are sitting in a crowded schoolroom, in front of a large, blank screen. In the back of the room, a teacher is using an old-fashioned slide projector. He turns it on, and we see a woman on the screen. A kid in the audience is a prankster, so when the teacher leaves the room, the kid jumps up with a marker, runs to the screen, and draws a mustache on the woman's face. When the teacher returns, he is understandably angry. So how does he clean away the mustache? Does he pull out the slide and wipe it away? Of course not. The slide, where the image exists, was unaffected. Instead, he goes and cleans the screen upon which the image was projected. Now let us say that your own brain is the slide projector, and the screen represents the reality all around you. If you want to actually affect your world, you must do so first from within instead of wasting time on the projection screen.

Dr. Joe Vitale says if you see something negative in another person or situation and do not try to remedy it starting with your own self-perception, "That's like trying to put your makeup on by looking in the mirror, but putting the makeup on the mirror. That's not going to help you." Vitale also wisely notes, "What you believe will filter all the available information around you to 'prove' your beliefs."

When R2-D2 projects the holographic form of Princess Leia with her plea, "Help me Obi-Wan Kenobi, you're my only hope," Leia does not actually exist, floating around in the air.

The information creating the hologram is actually inside R2-D2. Again, imagine yourself as R2-D2, and all of your experiential reality like the projection.

Redirecting Your Focus

Granted, this is a deep topic, but the point is really quite simple. *If your personal experience happens inside your head, then maybe you should focus on altering the picture in your head to alter the outward projection.* This is truly mind-blowing if you consider the implications. I am saying that you have even more control over your outer reality than you may have ever imagined. By changing the way you perceive a subject within your mind, you can change it in the so-called "external world," as well. Let me give you a personal example.

I once hired a man we'll call Bob to handle some of my business affairs. In the beginning, he was great and earned so much trust that little by little, due to my travel schedule, I granted him more and more access and control over aspects of my business. However, over time I gradually realized that Bob had a tendency toward paranoia. He became so protective of his position that he started acting aggressively toward others without reason. According to the Force, when you start to behave in a fearful, paranoid manner, even if there is nothing to be paranoid about, you will create behaviors in yourself that will, indeed, put you in jeopardy. As more and more people told me about their bad experiences, I started questioning Bob, and he was always overly sensitive and defensive. In time, when he finally became unprofessional and disrespectful toward me, I realized I had to sever my ties with him.

This was a tricky situation. I knew my business life would a real pain for a while, trying to get things back on track without him.

Bob knew this, too, and even made some threatening allusions to that effect. Regardless of the consequences, though, I knew the sooner I got this over with, the better. So I made arrangements for my final meeting with him.

The night before the meeting, I sat for a long time by myself, and quietly thought about Bob. At first I kept envisioning him at the meeting saying a lot of confrontational stuff, and I tried to think about my strategy to deal properly with anything he said, wherever the conversation might go. But after a while, I decided to try an experiment. What if I stopped imagining Bob this way? What if I just saw him being a nice guy, like he was when I originally met him, and we parted on peaceful terms? This felt good to me, and so I began to earnestly repaint Bob in my mind, and reimagine how things would go the next day.

As you can guess, when I met Bob the next day, I was floored by how my new, improved vision of Bob became a reality. He even said some of the actual words I had imagined him saying when I thought about things working out peacefully. All went as smoothly as one could imagine. We parted ways as friends, and he helped make the transition easy for me, though he could have been vengeful and not done so. I saw very quickly the true power of how what is formed in my head can be distinctly mirrored in the world around me.

Travels with the Frontal Lobe

Your brain is a miniature time machine. That's why you can mentally travel into the past to remember what you ate for lunch yesterday, or venture into the future to look at possible outcomes. Each time you make the decision whether or not to cross the road, the frontal lobe of the brain lights up as you imagine possible end results. The way you cross the road will depend on what vehicles are coming your way, their speed, and how they are spaced in relation to one another. It is in the frontal lobe where you can start focusing on how you expect certain events to turn out, and form them in your expectations before they happen.

The key is not only to think about using the Force to send out signals that change matter around you, but to also look inward, focusing on the actual interface within you. Some of the most energy-sensitive creatures are dogs. If you are a dog owner, you know how quickly a dog will pick up on your state of mind. If you are excited, your dog is excited. If you are sad, your dog is sad. After millennia of domestication, dogs are often very clear mirrors of their owners. As you may know (especially if you've ever watched shows like Cesar Millan's *Dog Whisperer*), you can generally control a dog's behavior by controlling your own. In other words, if you meet an aggressive dog, you can try waving your hand at the air and asking the Force to calm it. But you are much more likely to have success if you instead envision the dog being calm and conducting *yourself* as though it is.

Comprehending the mirror effect means that you must take even more responsibility for the role you personally play in how others treat you, and what opportunities come your way. Using the Force is not just about being able to impose your will on the world, but about evaluating yourself and considering the role you may play in the problems you have experienced. In fact, it's precisely Anakin Skywalker's efforts to use the Force to dominate others and impose his will that leads him to the dark side.

Do you find others far too critical? Then ask whether or not you, yourself, are too critical. Do you easily say negative things about other people whether you've met them or not? Then ask what among your life achievements qualifies you to be such a great and exceptional judge. You are apt to find, again and again, that many of the things you do not like in the world around you are actually being projected from you; you are just looking at them. Therefore, regardless of how powerful you may become as a manifestor, it will do you no good unless you are honest enough with yourself to drop your ego, be humble, and begin materializing goodness without judging all around you.

Unlearn What You Have Learned

A trusted friend once told me that rich people won't give away their money, and *that's* obviously why they're rich. I asked him, "How do you know how much they give away?" Of course, he didn't. He was just expressing a belief that he had apparently learned somewhere along the way. Some of the common, conventional wisdom you've accepted is very solid and true, and some of it is just outright myth. It is up to you to think maturely, to pause and examine all your "beliefs" once again, making a sincere effort to separate fact from fiction based upon what you actually, personally, know to be true.

One of the strangest scenes in the Star Wars movies is in *Episode V: The Empire Strikes Back*. After a hard day's training on Dagobah with Yoda, Luke suddenly feels a chill and senses there is something odd about a nearby hole in the ground. "That place is strong with the dark side of the Force," Yoda says with serious reservation. "A domain of evil it is. In you must go."

"What's in there?" Luke asks.

"Only what you take with you," Yoda replies.

Luke starts strapping on his weapons belt.

"Your weapons . . . you will not need them," Yoda assures him. Yet Luke, clearly skeptical of Yoda, attaches his weapons anyway and proceeds inside.

Once within this scary, underground cavern, Luke is stunned to come face to face with the tall, oppressive form of Darth Vader. They proceed to battle with lightsabers until Luke cuts off Vader's head. Luke looks at Vader's dismembered helmet, then, with a small explosion, the face of the mask incinerates, and behind it is Luke's own face. This whole scene is obviously a vision, an outward projection, mirroring what is deep within Luke's own mind.

The purpose of this scene is to illustrate the principles of the "mirror effect." I have often wondered how differently this might have turned out if Luke had not taken the weapons with him. Because he did take them, he produced the frightening confrontation *within himself*, illustrating the state of his mentality, both consciously and subconsciously. Again, as Yoda stated, all that existed inside the cavern was what Luke took with him.

From this scene, we can glean that, throughout your entire life, your experience depends largely on what you take with you. If you are working with the Force and producing changes, but they do not seem to be improving your life, it is your responsibility to pause, be introspective, and try to understand what you are hanging on to. Every single paradigm that exists within your head is what will, and must, determine what manifests. Even if you have a conscious idea of what you are trying to achieve, you cannot underestimate the power of the subconscious feelings that will determine just as greatly how things will turn out for you.

As the great Greek philosopher Socrates said, *gnothi seauton*— know thyself! This maxim is so important that it was inscribed in the forecourt of the Temple of Apollo at Delphi. The *Suda*, a tenth-century encyclopedia of Greek knowledge, says, "The proverb is applied to those whose boasts exceed what they are." It further explains that "know thyself" admonishes you to pay no attention to the opinions of the masses.

When you were born, you came into this world the same as everyone else. You knew nothing about who you were or what was happening. The world in which you were raised gave you the information you used to form your most fundamental opinions. But now, no matter who you are, how old you are, where you were born, or where you live, if you are intelligent enough to read and understand these words, you are smart enough to re-examine your life, experiences, and beliefs independently.

In the world of science we are still trying to find one universal theory that explains everything. At this moment, we are still far, far away from reaching that goal, but you often hear that opposites attract. For example, the north pole of a magnet attracts the south pole of a magnet, and vice versa. A negative electrical charge attracts a positive electrical charge, and vice versa. However, this is not true for all forces in nature. "Cohesion" is the term for how portions of substances like water (of which we are largely made) naturally attract each other. And gravitation, still one of the most mysterious and misunderstood forces in the universe, is the natural phenomenon by which all physical bodies attract each other. There is no doubt that this thing we call consciousness behaves like gravity, which is partially why we still do not have a firm grasp of how either work. The gravitational pull of your thoughts begins within your head. The incredible thing is that you possess this amazing ability called *will*, allowing you to shape and direct the nuances of what your inner mental gravity will attract.

No One Can Do Your Pushups for You

Using the Force is not just about being able to manifest things but about manifesting them wisely. The mirror effect is where your focus should start. Regardless of how comfortable you may or may not feel right now with who you are, it is always necessary to stop and brush up as often as possible. Great athletes such as Michael Jordan or Michael Phelps were not born with immense talent, relying solely upon it to carry them to triumphs. They continued to practice every day, honing their talent and keeping it as sharp and refined as possible. In fact, athletic trainers are often fond of saying, "No one can do your pushups for you." This is a thought-provoking message. No matter how rich and powerful you may be, it is absolutely true that no one can do your pushups for you. There are some things in life that you can, and must, only do for yourself, regardless of how talented you may be.

What Do You Take Inside?

Every day when you wake up to face the world, you are just like Luke Skywalker about to venture into the cavernous hole of self-reflection. Your whole life is only what you take inside with you. Remember, I am not suggesting that you can control the entire world inside your mind in some solipsistic way, but I am telling you that you are its co-creator. The sway you can have over the outcome of each day is far more monumental than you may have ever imagined. When you take each possible scenario and remake it in your head to your own liking, you can amaze yourself with the results. Yet you can only do this effectively if you are sending out positive energy by first doing all you can to improve yourself, repainting your self-identity in the same way.

One of the reasons the world loves Albert Einstein so much is that he understood intelligence is about more than just working out an equation. He realized that our scientific models are actually just representations of how the cosmos appears to work, and their relationship to the overall human experience. One of the great quotes attributed to him is, "We can't solve problems by using the same kind of thinking we used when we created them."

If you take a moment to think about that quote, and apply it to your own life, you will grasp how profound it truly is. Imagine all the problems you have right now. Are they regarding finances? Relationships? Health? Stability? Overall happiness? Why are these things problems for you? From where did they stem? If you take the time to introspect, you will discover that every problem came from a singular source and a way of thinking that began with a premise in your head at some time. You can therefore only expect to solve your problems by embracing a brand-new way of thinking, one more enlightened than what you've been using. Consider this for a moment: If you want to improve, then what you have been doing is *wrong*. This should be a welcome wake-up call for you, and you should feel grateful to come to this realization. Use it as an opportunity to become childlike again, and start reworking your world from the inside out. Let the new images in your mind project the fresh way people see you, and how you see others.

You cannot control the past, but you can control the future. When you are facing a problem, in order to address it properly, take a deep breath, relax, and, as the Jedi masters have always advised, *feel the Force flowing through you*. Only then can you court the universe properly to attain what will make you happy. In the next chapter, I will explain how you can do this effectively.

Chapter Eleven

Courting the Universe

"My ally is the Force,
and a powerful ally it is."

—Yoda, *Episode V: The Empire Strikes Back*

You are a human, capable of knowing only your own experience. Therefore, you are not able to fully know what the universe *is*, only what you *believe* it to be. So that is what is truly important. As Luke Skywalker (as every Jedi before him) trains to feel the Force not only within him, but also flowing *through* him, he is actually retraining his mind. But what is the fundamental nature of that retraining? It is to re-envision one's basic relationship with the universe.

Ancient and inferior animal instincts tend to make us feel somehow separated from all around us. However, a Jedi comes to first understand, then feel, then *know* from experience that he and the universe are one, in harmony. This is a wonderful realization, since it ultimately means that the same thought and sentiments that make you feel positive and generous are those that also make the universe feel positive and generous toward *you*. Grasping this is what separates the intellectual mind from the reactive.

Knowledge and Wisdom

In *Episode II*, Obi-Wan meets an informant/cook, named Dexter Jettster, to seek identification of an assassin's recovered dart. Obi-Wan explains that it didn't show up in the analysis archives. Jettster replies, "Those analysis droids only focus on symbols. I should think that you Jedi would have more respect for the difference between knowledge and *wisdom*."

What is that difference? Knowledge is simply knowing something, but wisdom is knowing the full context of something. This means that knowing you are part of an unimaginably powerful universe, grand enough to encompass all things, is different from grasping your personal relationship to that limitless might.

Therefore, how can you possibly get a handle on gaining the favor of the universal power? The answer is surprisingly and refreshingly simple. *You must mentally court the universe the way you would want to be courted.*

At first, this may seem utterly absurd. How on earth are you to court the universe? Again, this is ridiculously simple, yet its importance cannot be overstated. Whether or not you truly believe, right now, that the universe is a conscious entity all around you, start treating it that way. Say, "I love you," to the universe as often as possible. When you look at a beautiful sky, compliment the universe. If you're trying to woo a new lover, you might flatter her by talking about her stunning eyes or charming conduct. You should send out these same sentiments to creation all around you.

Impressing the Universe

Think of how you might conduct yourself in front of a multi-billionaire benefactor who is evaluating you. If you do well, a billion-dollar grant may be given to you. What things would you say to that person? What kind of behavior might you display before that person, in front of that individual? Even when you are all alone, pretend that you are impressing this giant, generous being who intends to help you and give you all you could ever imagine. Even if you have to force this conduct in the beginning, the more you do it, the more natural it will become. Best of all, the more rewards will begin flowing into your life. *Whether or not you believe the universe is a living, conscious being that cares about your attitude toward it, if you* behave *as though it is, it will also* behave *as though it is.* It works!

Imagine the universe becoming more and more impressed with you. The more you become in league with the cosmic forces, the more they will support you in every way. That is when the Force will start rushing through you like a river, and you will become a better and better conduit for its flow and sway upon matters around you. Better yet, as you become a true friend to the magnificent energy around you, you'll also become an ambassador for this energy to all other humans. It begins with an extremely effective technique I call *the magic of smiling*.

The Magic of Smiling

Smile as much, and as often, as possible. You will be astounded by the results. Each time you see yourself in a mirror, smile at yourself. Each time you see another person, smile at him or her. If you must, think of something happy in order to make it a wide, warm, genuine expression. If you begin every interaction you have with another person with a true smile, however challenging the situation may seem, incredibly positive things will happen.

I travel often, and zipping around the world on airplanes can be wrought with extremely stressful situations. On numerous occasions through the years, I have found myself in difficult predicaments. One time, for example, I was flying across the country from Nevada to North Carolina when a blizzard struck the east coast, grinding the airline schedules to a halt. I waited in line for hours to reach the airline counter. Since this was an act of nature and the airline was not obliged to offer free hotel accommodations, I watched travelers in front of me, over and over, shout at and insult the workers in dramatic displays. When I finally reached the counter, I was just the next number in line. I had no reason to think I would receive special treatment. However, I stepped up to the counter with a calm smile. The lady working had a puzzled expression on her face. Though I felt just as frustrated and stressed as everyone else, I chuckled and said kind, sympathetic things. Despite the airline policy, the lady granted me a nice, free hotel room for several days while I waited for the storm to subside. I have absolutely no doubt that this was due to the magic of smiling and my corresponding demeanor. I expressed and projected kindness, and that same kindness was reflected directly back to me.

Though it is important to be mindful of the Force and your relationship with it at all times, it is especially important to do so during episodes of stress. The more it seems things are unraveling around you, and those less-trained are descending into unregulated emotion and disarray, the more powerful you can be by sticking to your spiritual connections.

Be at Peace

In *Episode II: Attack of the Clones*, there is an action-packed scene where Obi-Wan and his apprentice Anakin are chasing an assassin, whizzing on airspeeders through the chaotic cityscape of Coruscant. The assassin finally crash-lands and runs into a club, with Anakin hot on her trail. Just as Anakin, adrenaline pumping, is about to chase her inside, Obi-Wan catches up and admonishes him. "Patience," advises Obi-Wan. "Use the Force. Think." With that, the two calmly make their way into the establishment and allow the Force to guide them on their mission. This scene exemplifies a potent message. Pause and tap into the enormous, universal power flowing through you. You will be far more successful acting as a channel than if you are distracted by limited, primitive instincts alone.

A person who is aware of the Force flowing through herself is always at peace. That's because there is no individual problem more powerful than the collective, harmonious forces that keep our world constantly moving forward in perfect balance. To become aware of that energy pulsing through you and supporting you like a timeless cushion will naturally melt your expression into a smile, and those around you will feel rays of confidence beaming from you. This is the nature of true charisma.

The word "charisma" is often overused. It's true that even people with troubled lives, like some actors or politicians, may still have charisma. Why is this? It's because they are able to channel it at certain times, but not others. They open the switch to the Force when they are on the spot—in front of the camera or on the stage of a debate—but then turn it off. Why is that? It's because they either never properly cleared the mental negativity from their past, or their charisma attracted toxic people and distractions that they allowed to remain. That is why your relationship with the universe must always, *always* be your top consideration. It must be first and foremost in your mind and spirit. If you maintain the proper, respectful, admiring perspective of the universe, you will perpetually remain in good hands.

Never Appear Needy

While envisioning the universe as a being you want to impress each moment, one you expect to fulfill your desires, one of the worst things you can do is appear needy. Imagine if you were a genie, but you could grant a wish to only ten people. Obviously, everyone on Earth would love to have a wish granted. How would you wisely choose the best ten wishes to grant? The first thing you would do is listen to the requests. Some might seem trivial and others more important, but one of the things you would consider would be the long-term impact of the fulfilled wish. In other words, what wishes would present the highest odds for long-term positive impact, getting the most bang for the buck?

To make this simple, let's focus on money again. Let's say one person comes to you and says, "Great Genie, I have been poor my entire life. I beg you for a million dollars." Another approaches and says, "Great Genie, I have been an entrepreneur for ten years. My business has grown, and I would love to have a million dollars to grow it more." You might worry that giving a million dollars to someone who has never had money would be a mistake. That person might not understand the responsibilities of handing such a large sum and would lose it quickly on trivial things, like many people who hit a lottery. But the entrepreneur might understand money enough to take the million and use it more wisely, growing it into a larger sum over time that would create opportunities to benefit many more. Obviously, such a scenario would vary greatly based on the individuals involved, but you can see how appearing needy can create doubts. Since business succeeds when there is a mutually beneficial exchange among the business and others, the experienced entrepeneur should have a deeper understanding of how that money can be used over time to benefit more than himself.

The problem of neediness also plays out in the world of romantic dating. Most people have encountered needy suitors at some point in their lives. If a person wants to be your partner but seems too needy, he gives the impression that no one else is interested in him. You can't help but ask yourself why this is. On the other hand, if a suitor has a calm, relaxed demeanor and does not place uncomfortable pressure on you, that keeps the entire situation more relaxed and increases the chances you will see this person as someone who is confident and more worthy of your attention. That is why you should never "appear" needy to the universe. Whenever there is a problem, simply feel confident the universe will help you overcome it. Why? Because you and the universe have a great, mutually respectful, loving relationship.

Qui-Gon Finds a Pod Racer

We see this attitude in *Episode I: The Phantom Menace*, when Qui-Gon Jinn and his crew are stranded on Tatooine. In need of parts to repair the ship, Qui-Gon is searching for money. Obi-Wan tells him they have nothing on board valuable enough to buy the proper supplies. Instead of stressing out and begging the Force for help, Qui-Gon calmly replies, "All right. I'm sure another solution will present itself." This moment exemplifies the Jedi's trusting relationship with the Force and the universe. He not only remains calm and confident, but we later see that he must have known this situation was presented for a reason. By staying on Tatooine, he develops his friendship with young Anakin, eventually freeing the boy from slavery and taking him away to become a Jedi.

"Our meeting was not a coincidence," Qui-Gon tells Anakin's mother. "Nothing happens by accident." This is a liberating mindset. If you know your intentions are positive, and yet obstacles still arise, see them as opportunities. This is how the universe will help you in ways you do not expect, and it happens when you trust in the Force instead of trying to bend it to your will. Remember, the overall language of the universe is synchronicity. It is older, wiser, and vaster. It knows more than you.

Sometimes, people who use the Force are confused. They do their best to follow all of the guidelines they read about in books and hear about in lectures, yet their wishes do not come true. It is easy for those folks to simply toss the entire technique aside and call it hogwash. Of course, those kinds of people never really understood it in the first place. There always remains an open dialogue between you and the universe. If you are not getting the results you desire, then you should rethink the way you are presenting yourself rather than tossing the baby out with the bathwater.

It is never too late to re-examine where you are, what you want, and how you have been asking for it. Once you state very clearly what you desire, it is not necessary to incessantly repeat it and obsess over it. It *is* important for you to keep your desire in mind as often as possible, because you are constantly sending out the signals that are actively shaping it each moment—not because you are making a demand to Santa Claus again and again until you annoy him into fulfilling it.

Flattery

You've probably heard the old adage that "flattery will get you everywhere." It's a bit much to state it will get you everywhere, but it will definitely take you a long way. Flattery focuses on the things that are positive about a person or thing. Unfortunately, many interpret flattery as giving exaggerated compliments in order to achieve some selfish goal. In fact, it should be about transmitting praise as a courtesy that will, inevitably, create a positive reaction. This is good for all parties involved. Flattery is especially important as you court the universe.

On numerous occasions, I have enjoyed a breathtaking sunset on a warm, tropical beach. Each time I watch the dwindling light shimmer on the water, as the epic sky above transforms into vibrant, mystical colors, I think to myself: "If I were the creator of this, how could I do any better and produce anything more beautiful?" Billions of sunsets occurred before I was born. How fortunate I am to be there, at that moment, to witness such an overwhelming thing. I am incapable of comprehending the power that created this—greater than any human king in history—and yet I feel reassured to be in league with that power. And then, a damn mosquito bites me!

Isn't it weird that the same natural forces responsible for the magnificence of a sunset are those that have allowed these little blood-sucking insects to persist and spread illness to millions each year? We must accept that what seem to us to be all-powerful beings and things have both good and bad attributes. If I chose to focus on mosquitoes, I could curse the power that made that sunset almost every night of every year. But what would the result be? I would only be transmitting negative energies, which would reflect back to me instead of the positive ones I want. In fact, those mosquitos provide a rich diet to the colorful birds that sing relaxing songs and spread the seeds that sprout into the plants I eat to survive. You must *resign* yourself to the fact there is a greater power than you, and that power works with purpose. I cannot snap my fingers and rid the world of mosquitoes anyway, so why should I focus on that annoyance instead of flattering the universe for those qualities I find so immensely wonderful?

You must view each human being, and every scenario you encounter, in the same way. It is not a matter of turning a blind eye to the things that seem to be working against you. It is a practical matter of understanding how the laws of the universe directly affect you. Your brain, and the research of humans before you were born, have shown us that you exist as an individual transmitter. Focusing on the positive, and complimenting it, does not make you a naive optimist, rather an educated realist. Flatter the universe as often as possible each day, and you will be rewarded for that flattery.

As a conduit for universal energy and a creator yourself, your brain and mind are perfectly suited to taking the elements around you and converting them into what you desire. The human mind has conceived of machines that utterly transform the basic components of nature at will. How profound it is that an icemaker can take water, the most plentiful substance on earth, and convert it into icy cubes on demand. The human mind took that same substance and heated it for steam, powerful enough to power engines to haul tons of mined material across our lands to build great cities. Your impact on the environment is profound. Yet it all begins with a creative relationship between you and everything around you, appreciating what is there for what it is, and then visualizing how it can be transformed through your brain—the most complex and mysterious organ known to mankind.

Your Mind As the Ultimate Tool

The relationship between you, the universe, and your ability to influence the medium of reality is the crux of using the Force. In fact, this is demonstrated in an interesting way in *Episode I: The Phantom Menace*. Circumstances trapped Qui-Gon on Tatooine so he could discover Anakin and take him away. However, there comes a crucial point when the matter of whether or not Anakin can be freed depends upon a single wager. The businessman Watto, a gruff flying creature who owns Anakin and his mother, is willing to gamble over whether the boy or his mother should be given to Qui-Gon.

"We'll let fate decide," Watto suggests. "I just happen to have a chance cube here." He pulls out a die with some faces painted red and others painted blue. "Blue, it's the boy; red, his mother," says Watto. Qui-Gon nods in confident agreement.

Watto rolls the die. As it passes by, Qui-Gon slyly waves his hand, and the die lands on blue. We are given the clear impression that Qui-Gon used his telekinetic Jedi power to ensure the die landed the way he wanted, in favor of him getting Anakin. However, this brings up an interesting question. If all the circumstances, up to that point, had conspired (even outside of Qui-Gon's knowledge) to make sure Qui-Gon fulfilled the destiny of taking Anakin, why was it now necessary for Qui-Gon to become so "hands-on" and directly involved in fulfilling the destiny? If Qui-Gon had not raised his hand, would the die have fallen on red, thereby changing the entire fate of the galaxy? We can never know the answer to this. However, what was demonstrated here was the nature of the partnership between the Jedi and the Force. In the beginning, Qui-Gon did not see the big picture, but he trusted that the Force did. Once he finally also perceived the big picture, the Force needed him to act as the channel to realize it. The end result is a symbiotic relationship in which both the man and the universe work in tandem to move the agenda forward. This kind of relationship can only arise from mutual respect and the harmony of mutual self-interest.

Chance

The world loves, and is forever indebted to, the French chemist and microbiologist Louis Pasteur. In the nineteenth century, he pioneered the principles of vaccination and other techniques to preserve our bodies from a wide variety of germs. One of his famous quotes is, "Chance favors the prepared mind." Chance, in general, plays a fascinating role in how one relates to the design and form of the world.

One of the oldest manuscripts in existence is the Chinese *I Ching*, or *Book of Changes*. It was produced more than 3,000 years ago and explains a system of divination known as *cleromancy*. The concept is that a group of objects, like plant stalks, coins, pebbles, beans, or bones can be tossed onto the ground, and then "read" based upon the manner in which they land. The reading commonly regards the future outcome of some perplex situation, or a prognosis of the current state of affairs. Also known as the casting of lots, cleromancy has been used by virtually all cultures and is even referenced in the Bible. The popular tarot deck, used by Europeans since the mid-fifteenth century, is also thought to operate via this principle. However it is done, an expert interprets the way the pieces fall or organize, and delivers a message. It is believed that what some would simply call random placement is never random at all, and that there are always forces guiding the way matter behaves. To believe otherwise would imply there could be a distinct effect without a distinct cause, and this, of course, makes little sense. In short, cleromancy is like dropping a leaf, and watching the way it falls to determine the direction of the wind.

Look for Patterns

Whether or not these specific methods of divination indeed work to give us insight on the hidden forces behind life, the concept is a great reference for you. Those people who have been considered experts in interpreting the way these items are arranged base their analysis on many hundreds or thousands of years of trial and error by previous generations. Since you are a unique individual, you must use your previous experiences in life to interpret all the events around you, being aware of how circumstances may be leading you to certain outcomes. *Treat everything within and around you like a massive handful of I Ching coins constantly falling into place.* Learn to read them each second, informing you of the situations and prospects constantly developing. Move toward the things you want to experience, and away from those you do not.

In order for you to maximize your own ability to read the environment, you must be aware at all times. This is a disheartening proposition for some, since it requires work. It's much easier to lie around watching TV and eating potato chips than to constantly analyze everything around you. Fortunately, there is a wonderful tradeoff. If your relationship with the universe is positive and you maintain awareness, you can be guided, if you so choose, toward situations that will grant you relaxation, fulfillment, and joy.

There are really two different kinds of relaxation. One comes from being passive and lazy, the other from being actively engaged in things that bring you peace and joy. Since, whether you like it or not, you are in this world to be a creator, you will find time and time again that the process of creating something positive will bring you the ultimate peace. This is why you must strive to keep your connection to the universe—what many call the *source*—as direct, honest, and mutually loving as possible. If you do so, you will be astounded by how interactive the universe will be, directing actions toward you.

Don't Miss the Signals

In *The Millions Within*, David Neagle provides the parable of a deeply religious man who lived on a floodplain. Three of his neighbors came over to alert him of a flood warning and help him pack and transport him away. "No," he said, refusing their help. "My

Lord will save me." A short while later, as the flood waters poured in, a sheriff's department truck pulled up with a megaphone, begging him to come with them. "No," the man shouted. "I'm fine. My Lord will save me." Later, as the flood waters rose above his house and he waded in the treacherous streams, a rescue helicopter flew overhead, lowering a ladder. "No," he insisted, "my Lord will save me!" And then he drowned. Minutes later, the man stood wet and weary before St. Peter. "I have been a good, God-fearing man my entire life! Why did the Lord not save me?" he asked angrily.

"Let me check on this and see," replied St. Peter. He thumbed through the record and said, "Ah! But God tried, you see. He sent you three neighbors, a sheriff's car, and a helicopter!"

The purpose of this story is to illustrate the *realistic* components of how the universe will contact and communicate with you. It will do so through circumstantial developments, and it relies on your intelligence and perceptiveness to realize the opportunities that are being presented. The success of this communication depends on clarity in both directions. Consider that everything you see around you, however small or giant, is a message you are expected to properly interpret. You cannot await the manifestation of some angelic being that will give you clear instructions. Just as you cannot expect your communication with a pet dog to transcend basic commands, you cannot assume the vast powers of the cosmos will give you direct, literal information on your own scale. Every time someone takes a moment to give you advice, or a situation points toward a logical outcome, you should pay attention and be mindful of what this information may mean for you, at the very least. Whether you perceive it as positive or negative at the time, understand that it has come into your life at that specific moment for a reason. It may be to show you something that is good or bad, accurate or inaccurate, but it should always be appreciated as educational, at least. You must receive that information fully so you can process its greater context and, based upon it, make wiser decisions.

Put Down Your Ego

The primary obstacle to receiving new, educational input is your ego. For our purposes, *ego* is defined as your own sense of self-importance. It is crucial for you to feel self-important; hence the existence of your self-esteem. However, if you embrace your ego as a singular entity, entirely separate from all the forces around it, you will miss all the things that will enrich your ego and expand your life in successful directions. In fact, you will feel as if your ego is often in conflict with your world. You may believe your ego is more advanced than your environment and thereby being subjected to incessant stupidity. Or you may think it is inferior to your environment, forcing you into a defensive mode. Whatever the case, you are separating yourself more and more from the universe, leading toward bad things.

Humble balance, personal independence, and sincere open-mindedness are the keys to a prosperous and personally rewarding relationship with your positive universe. In Ancient Greece, the Temple of Apollo at Delphi also bore the inscription *Meden Agan*, meaning "nothing in excess." Yet all throughout history humans have been plagued by excessive feelings of being superior or inferior, always leading to the same place. It is a powerful domain, full of incredible achievement, but it is always self-destructive. In Star Wars, it is called—simply and appropriately—the dark side.

Chapter Twelve

Beware of the Dark Side

"Fear is the path to the dark side.
Fear leads to anger. Anger leads to hate.
Hate leads to suffering."

—Yoda, *Episode I: The Phantom Menace*

Everything you have learned thus far can slip into evil. Let me tell you the story of the *real* Darth Vader.

Many of the world's ancient texts feature the concept and lessons of the Law of Attraction in a karmic sense. Though the word "karma" is rooted in the Sanskrit language, all cultures, religions, and philosophies support it in some way. The Hindu *Brihadaranyaka Upanishad*, composed thousands of years ago, states, "Truly, one becomes good through good action, and evil through evil action." In the Bible, Galatians 6:7 states "Whatsoever a man soweth, that shall he reap." The very first time the actual phrase "Law of Attraction" is known to have appeared in print was in 1877. In her book, *Isis Unveiled: A Master-Key to the Mysteries of Ancient and Modern Science and Technology*, Helena Blavatsky wrote, "By whatsoever name the physicists may call the energizing principle in nature . . . if the law of attraction is admitted as governing one, why should it be excluded from influencing the other?"

Helena Blavatsky, often referred to as Madame Blavatsky, was born in 1831 in what is now the Ukraine and died in London in 1891 at the age of fifty-nine. She was a world-famous philosopher and occultist who traveled the globe investigating spiritual cultures and esoteric mysteries. Her friends included inventors such as Thomas Edison and astronomer Camille Flammarion. In 1875, she was a founder of the Theosophical Society, an institute devoted to metaphysical research and publishing. Blavatsky herself defined Theosophy as "the archaic Wisdom-Religion, the esoteric doctrine once known in every ancient country having claims to civilization."

The Thule Society and Adolf Hitler

In 1918, the year World War I ended, a strange group was formed in Germany called the Thule Society. Created by some of the wealthiest and most elite men in Germany, including industrial barons, philosophers, politicians, scientists, and visionaries, it took its name from a mythical northern country in Greek legend (similar to Scandinavia). Members believed their Aryan race had descended from deities. In order to join the society, prospective members had to sign a "blood declaration of faith" stating, "The signer hereby swears to the best of his knowledge and belief that no Jewish or coloured blood flows in either his or in his wife's veins, and that among their ancestors are no members of the coloured races." Due to the members' general interest in the mystical, the works of Madame Blavatsky were standard, if not required, reading.

The wealthy Thule Society became the central sponsor of a fledgling political party called the Deutsche Arbeiterpartei (DAP). That party was later reorganized by a young man named Adolf Hitler into the National Socialist German Workers' Party (NSDAP or Nazi Party). It has frequently been suggested that Hitler usually kept a copy of Madame Blavatsky's magnum opus, *The Secret Doctrine: The Synthesis of Science, Religion and Philosophy*, on his nightstand. Do you think it a coincidence that Adolf Hitler probably read, before drifting off to sleep at night, the work of the first person to publish the phrase "Law of Attraction"?

Hitler was born the fourth of six children into a lower-middle-class Austrian family in 1889. As a young man, he was a common laborer and art school reject. He volunteered as a solider of the Bavarian Army in WWI and was wounded. After the war, at almost thirty years of age with no formal education or career prospects, there was no indication that he would ever have a great impact on society. In fact, still a member of the army, he was assigned to spy on the up-and-coming German Worker's Party (DAP). It was at the DAP where Hitler met Dietrich Eckart, an associate of the Thule Society. The Thule Society believed a "German Messiah" would appear, and after hearing Hitler give a rousing speech Eckart introduced him to the Thule as a good candidate. There is no doubt that Hitler was immersed into an occult world where the magic of mental manifestation was stressed. Less than fifteen years later he would be the dictator of Germany and its provinces, one of the most powerful leaders the world has ever known. In 1939, six years after coming to power as Chancellor, he declared in a speech about Britain that he would "brew them a devil's drink," and he invaded Poland. World War II began, and he damn near took over the entire world. Fortunately, his unimaginable reign of terror ended in 1945 as he trembled in a bunker below Berlin, ear-shattering bombs blasting above. His wife chewed on a cyanide capsule, and he shot himself in the head. Because of his actions, up to 85 million people had died—and the United States unleashed the destructive power of atomic bombs—making World War II the deadliest conflict in human history. Hitler was a powerful manifestor, who used the Force for the darkest of purposes.

Most of the time, when you read about the Law of Attraction, the emphasis is placed on all the positive things one can accomplish by properly implementing its techniques. However, we would be terribly remiss to not acknowledge that those same techniques can be used to achieve destructive goals. It is a stark reminder that the Law is truly impartial. The Law is simply a mechanism by which your mind affects the reality around you, and it can be used for evil just as easily as it can be used for good. However, there are some things each person must consider.

What You Project Will Always Come Back to You

Hitler used his understanding of how to manifest, and produced anguish. It was clear that, eventually, that same anguish would return to him. That is why his entire creation imploded and self-destructed. He was delusional enough to think he could manifest an evil empire that would sustain itself for 1,000 years. However, as you can see from his life, the repercussions came quickly. From the time he began organizing his thoughts of manifestation with the Thule Society to the time he committed suicide, approximately twenty-five years passed. Granted, twenty-five years is a long time; yet it is only about one-quarter of a current human life span.

Hitler expended an enormous amount of energy during that time, shook all of human history in the most horrendous way, and then collapsed into utter despair, all within that quarter-century. Though Hitler was fifty-six when he died, he looked and acted much older; the stress he had created wore his body and spirit down at an accelerated rate. One can indeed use the Force to materialize horrible things, but there is always a dramatic cost to the one who projects it, aside from the collateral damage.

The Cost of the Dark Side

Star Wars gives several examples of the terrible price the dark side exacts from its adherents. Senator Palpatine becomes the Emperor, but his face and body are withered in the process. Anakin turns to the dark side, but in the combat with Obi-Wan his legs are slashed from under him and much of his body is literally burned away. In the end, as Obi-Wan says, "He's more machine than man." Everyone in the Star Wars galaxy suffers for allowing Palpatine to slyly obtain unchecked power. We have all heard the old adage, "All tyranny needs to gain a foothold is for people of good conscience to remain silent." Or, put more simply, "All a bad person needs to become a leader is for the good people to do nothing."

Each of us is responsible for looking after the state of our societies.

Take Action!

In the original Star Wars movie, *Episode IV: A New Hope*, Han Solo represents the practical man who relies on technology, conventional wisdom, and common sense to live life and solve problems. Darth Vader represents the dark wizard, in touch with overwhelming "magical" powers, who cannot be defeated. During the climax of the movie, Luke Skywalker is part of a group of X-wing starfighters hoping to destroy the Death Star, an enormous, moon-sized space station with one small weak spot. As Luke zooms toward it, preparing to use the Force to guide his shot into the vulnerable port, Darth Vader pilots a TIE fighter, hot on Luke's trail. "The Force is strong with this one," Vader says, as he gets ready to take out Luke's fighter. But then Han Solo unexpectedly appears in the *Millennium Falcon* and fires on Vader's craft. "What?!" exclaims Vader, as Solo's shot sends Vader's fighter spiraling into space. "You're all clear, kid!" yells Solo, and Luke sends a blast perfectly into the tiny vulnerable spot of the Death Star. The Empire's space station explodes into a billion points of light, finally shifting the tide of the galactic war in favor of the Rebellion.

This is an extremely important moment in the Star Wars series. We see a non-Jedi completely disrupt an experienced Jedi during a crucial moment. There is a realistic component at play here. It demonstrates that nothing is more important than taking action. The world is full of potential, but *somebody* has to be the one to intervene and channel the potential energy into kinetic energy. You are either master *of* mind or mastered *by* mind. Whether right or wrong, people who get up, get out, and do something are always going to have the upper hand. There is a great deal of power in simply being active, however untrained one may be. And yet, you must be wise about the timing. When Luke left Dagobah to face Vader before his training was complete, he lost his hand in the battle. Of course, he also learned the painful truth about his origin at that time, that Vader was his biological father.

In the mind of Darth Vader, we can imagine that Han Solo, a blue-collar smuggler, is at the opposite end of the spectrum from a trained Jedi. Vader would arrogantly brush him off the radar as a direct threat. Yet, it's precisely because he ignores Han that the smuggler gains the upper hand at that pivotal moment. Ironically, it is Vader's sole focus on Luke at that time that proves to be his greatest weakness. In fact, this overall scenario explains a lot about how and why those who use the Force's dark side are often perceived as more powerful than those who use it for right.

Defining Good and Evil

Philosophers have always struggled with defining good and evil. In my opinion, it's quite clear. Evil equals complete and absolute self-centeredness, without any regard for how that self-centeredness affects others. As it turns out, evil people are historically much more focused than good people. Why? Because they can afford focus, since it takes less overall effort to go after low-hanging fruit. They are also not expending extra energy on caring for others. Evil people are in many respects evolutionary throwbacks to an age when we were more animalistic. On television nature programs you can watch a pride of lions tear apart a gazelle; that's a natural act for them. An evil person sees the strong destroying the weak as just as natural; therefore, he believes it should be just as accepted. Once he no longer feels it is necessary to deal with the full implications of such an act, he is freed, in his mind, to focus on more of this ruthless domination.

Evil people feel they can justify their aggressive behavior, based both on how lower creatures act and how they themselves have been treated. Fortunately, though, negative thoughts are ultimately weaker than positive thoughts. If a dark side Jedi goes up against a light side Jedi, the Jedi of the light will always, in the long run, win. That is because the light is lasting energy, and the dark is a dwindling form of that energy. As Luke trains on Dagobah, he asks Yoda, "Is the dark side stronger?"

"No, no, no . . ." snaps Yoda. "Quicker, easier, more seductive."

Reactions of the Human Body

A controversial form of kinesiology, the scientific study of human movement, is kinesthesiology. It is a largely subjective muscle-testing technique. The idea is that your body possesses an inherent truth and integrity detector. When you are subjected to truths, your muscles grow stronger, and when you are subjected to lies and deception, your muscles grow weaker. A kinesthesiologist will ask his client to hold her arm out and answer a question while another person presses down upon the arm. So, for example, I might have you hold your arm out and ask you, "Are you from the planet Earth?" You would say, "Yes," and at that point, I would press down on your arm and feel a certain level of resistance, or muscle strength. Next, I might ask, "Are you from Mars?" If you said, "Yes" (knowing this to be untrue), and I pressed down on your arm, it would collapse much more easily because your muscles would be weakened by your lie. This kind of exercise is fun for demonstrations but involves too many variables to be scientific. Nonetheless, the general concept seems to be valid when observing human behavior.

When a person achieves a goal playing a game and exclaims "Yes!" his or her fist often punches into the air enthusiastically. When have you seen the same happen when someone shouts "No!"? In fact, people screaming "No!" usually fall to their knees dramatically, weakened in every way. As silly as it may seem at first, positive things awaken and strengthen us, and negative things weaken us. In the pitiful scene in *Episode III: Revenge of the Sith* when the Emperor tells the newly created Darth Vader that he killed Padmé, Vader screams "*No!*" as his body draws back in weakness.

Adolf Hitler was the real Darth Vader. He was a man who understood the principles of manifestation—the Force—and used them. If he had chosen to work in the light, he could have been one of the greatest forces for good ever known to humankind. Instead, he chose to use his talent to enhance the dark side. He might have looked up the chain of human evolution and envisioned a new era in which humanity would tend to unite and leave ideas of class and racism behind. Instead, he stupidly clung to the past, insensitive to the direction of the world. In 1934, he said to a British correspondent, "At the risk of appearing to talk nonsense, I tell you that the

National Socialist movement will go on for 1,000 years! . . . Don't forget how people laughed at me fifteen years ago when I declared that one day I would govern Germany. They laugh now, just as foolishly, when I declare that I shall remain in power!"

It is a good thing that the dark side is weaker than the light. All throughout history, again and again, the light has won—hence the freedom you have, right now, to read these words. If there is something in your mind that is pulling you toward the dark side, know that it will not succeed, and all it can bring you is great personal suffering and regret. There is nothing but the light, and the absence of the light. George Lucas knew all of this from studying Hitler's regime, and he incorporated some specific elements into his story based on Germany's military history.

The term "stormtrooper" was used by Lucas to describe the common foot soldiers of the Galactic Empire. The standard Imperial stormtrooper wears white body armor and a white helmet, with black joints and accents. And yet the term "stormtrooper" comes straight from body-armored specialist soldiers of the German Army in World War I. They were called *Sturmtruppen* (assault troops) or sometimes "thrust troops" or "shock troops," there to infiltrate enemy lines with overwhelming power, instilling dramatic fear in the enemy. Calling the Empire's front line stormtroopers makes it clear that Lucas was inspired by the Nazis as he developed the look and idea of Darth Vader, his soldiers, and the Empire's regime.

Evil and Light

If the dark world surrounding Darth Vader was a reflection of Adolf Hitler, what does that say about the good side, the light? I have defined evil as absolute self-centeredness, without any regard for how that self-centeredness affects others. Does that mean good-ness is the opposite: selflessness with complete regard for how that selflessness affects others? No.

Good is, very simply, "overcoming evil." Yet, the challenge in discerning good from evil comes in developing awareness—the ability to clearly see an issue from all sides and weigh each facet wisely. Throughout history, most people who acted wickedly were able to convince themselves that they were, in fact, doing the right thing. We have all heard that "the road to hell is paved with good intentions." This saying is thought to have originated with Saint Bernard of Clairvaux, a French abbot who lived from 1090 to 1153. It is a powerful and frightening statement. How can you know whether or not you are working in the darkness or the light?

It reminds me of the concept of insanity. You can never trust someone who says, "I'm not crazy," or "I'm not stupid." That's because a crazy person would not necessarily know whether or not he is crazy, and a stupid person would not necessarily know whether or not she is stupid. Sanity entails the realization that you might be obliviously insane, and intelligence entails the realization that you may not be smart enough to understand you are, in fact, unwise. The Star Wars movies explore this challenging territory as we watch how Anakin, a promising child with pure intentions, slowly transitions into one of the galaxy's greatest villains.

Trusting Elders

In *Episode III: Revenge of the Sith*, Palpatine summons Anakin for a private conference. At that point, despite suspicions regarding Palpatine's agenda, Anakin still trusts him as an elder leader. Palpatine tells Anakin his intelligence units have discovered the location of General Grievous, a figure perceived as a common enemy. "At last, we'll be able to capture that monster and end this war," says Anakin.

"I would worry about the collective wisdom of the council if they didn't select you for this assignment; you're the best choice, by far," says Palpatine. By saying this, Palpatine begins the process of confusing Anakin about who is righteous, and who is betraying whom.

"The Jedi use their power for good," says Anakin.

"Good is a point of view, Anakin," replies Palpatine. From there, the elder man—knowing that Anakin, plagued by visions and concerned about the possible death of his wife—tempts him with an astounding power. Palpatine asks if Anakin has ever heard of Darth Plagueis the Wise, subject of a Sith legend. He explains that Darth Plagueis learned the power of overcoming death and implies that Anakin can also learn this skill, but *only* from the Sith. Therein is the temptation that ultimately moves Anakin from the light into the dark.

The lesson in this scene is about more than the danger of giving in to one's desires. It's also about blindly trusting one's elders. We all know that elders are due respect, yet you must realize that being a good person is far better than simply being old. In fact, elders may sometimes be the biggest threat to positive change. Longer life has often afforded them the ability to accrue more wealth and name-recognition that can be used as enticements, but these things should be treated with great caution. Because of their age, elders are sometimes more concerned with maintaining their own relevance and power, as opposed to nourishing the long-term welfare of the world.

Consider that a little more than 300 years ago, twenty people were tortured and executed in Salem, Massachusetts, on baseless charges of being witches. A hundred and fifty years ago, many Americans owned slaves. Less than 100 years ago, women could not vote in the United States. And about fifty years ago, legal racial segregation still existed in America.

The point is that, despite what the media often tell us, with time we are improving as a fair, enlightened society. We cannot and should not ever underestimate the mindset of the young in determining the right side of the Force. Age certainly has its benefits, but, sadly, not everyone becomes nicer or better with age. Nor can you rely solely on the traditions of your ancestors to move you in the right direction. Determining right from wrong is an ageless dilemma, and it is crucial for you to not only possess a clear mind, capable of imagining a scenario from many perspectives, but to also be able to use your feelings. It is easier to sway one intellectually than it is emotionally, so *beware of those who focus on persuading and tempting you with isolated intellectual arguments, even if they try to tie in an emotional component of your life.*

A person might say, "In my eighty years, every rottweiler I've met has been mean." However, that does not prove that all rottweilers are indeed mean. Keep an open mind when weighing someone's opinion. All pigeons are birds, but not all birds are pigeons. This type of basic logic, illustrated by Venn diagrams is, sadly enough, too often missing in the world's fundamental education these days.

In *Episode III: Revenge of the Sith*, as he battles furiously on a bed of lava with his one-time friend and Jedi mentor, Obi-Wan shouts, "Anakin, Chancellor Palpatine is evil!"

"From my point of view, the Jedi are evil!" Anakin exclaims.

"Well, then you are lost!" Obi-Wan cries, anguish in his voice. After warning Anakin to stop fighting to no avail, Obi-Wan chops off Anakin's legs with his lightsaber. Crawling pitifully on the ground, his eyes red with rage, Anakin screams, "I hate you!" Flames consume his body, and the personality "Anakin" disappears as he becomes "Darth Vader" before our eyes. From there, he can only survive by being more machine than human.

Though the story is merely a movie, it accurately depicts a reality: individuals can morph into darkness. Though we can view Darth Vader as part of Hollywood's black-and-white division between good guys and bad guys, we can also see here how a character with essential, inherent goodness—someone with whom we have sympathized—can still give in to evil seduction. One might imagine, while watching this scene, that Anakin has realized the error of his ways, but if he has, it's too late to reverse course.

You can slip over to the dark side. I'm not suggesting for a minute that this would have the same impact as Hitler or Darth Vader. But you should see the potential variables in your own, real life. Even if you have followed all the guidelines in this book to capture the positive power and promising future that is yours for the taking, you can lose your proper perspective. You may become a very powerful Jedi, working in the light, and then, over time, begin using your power to achieve dark goals. How do you avoid this?

Vigilance

Another great quote, often attributed to Thomas Jefferson, is "Eternal vigilance is the price of liberty." When you think of this, you might understandably think about the liberty of a country or society. Instead, stop and think how this relates to your own freedom. I wish I could tell you that once you fully understand and implement the practical guidelines in this book, you will achieve a spiritual plateau that allows you to sail through life and effortlessly reap its rewards. However, the frustrating truth is that every day you must put forth effort to discern what is right from what is wrong, and project your energy and intentions in the proper direction. Life is full of so many variables that there is no one rule that applies to every situation. But, generally speaking, every mentally healthy person must possess some barometer for righteousness and caring. Otherwise, our civilizations would have self-destructed long ago.

I often find it incredible that traffic flows as well as it does every day in towns and cities all around this world. As simple as this may seem at first, this is a good indication of how most people follow the rules and conduct themselves in a way to preserve their own lives and the lives of others. This is remarkable, considering the number of people barreling around in machines capable of killing someone in an instant.

The Golden Rule

"Do unto others as you would have them do unto you" has been called the Golden Rule since the seventeenth century in Europe, but it has been found in some form in the earliest texts of ancient Babylon and in almost all cultures since then. Rushworth Kidder, who founded the Institute for Global Ethics in 1990, noted that the Golden Rule's conceptual framework appears prominently in many religions, including "Hinduism, Buddhism, Taoism, Judaism, Zoroastrianism, and the rest of the world's major religions." One might easily argue that it is the underlying thread in determining proper behavior from improper, or, to be more explicit, good from evil.

Basic as it may seem, implementing the Golden Rule is much simpler to think about than to practice. The animalistic instinct we each possess is an ever-present force, continually drawing us backward in our evolution. We cannot help that we are dealing with genes rooted millions of years in the past, which are constantly tugging at our emotions and outlook on life. However, part of becoming more advanced creatures is acknowledging the presence of these feelings, and understanding that all humans have them. This is something that comes partly with age, as we get to know more and more people, especially from different cultures and backgrounds, and realize all the attributes we share in common.

Gossip and Useless Knowledge

How do you do your best to be a good purveyor of the Force and not use whatever power you have for the dark and self-destructive side? For one thing, as you consider any scenario, always stop to imagine yourself in the other person's position. This applies not only to the individual you are directly facing, but also to anyone who might be related to the conversation. There is a story about Socrates and his approach to gossip, possibly apocryphal, that has circulated for years. Here's one version:

In ancient Greece one day Socrates, the great philosopher, was approached by an excited man who said, "Socrates, do you know what I just heard about one of your students?"

"Wait a moment," Socrates replied. "Before you tell me, I'd like you to pass a little test. It's called the Test of Three. Before you talk to me about my student, let's take a moment to test what you're going to say. The first test is Truth. Have you made absolutely sure that what you are about to tell me is true?"

"No," the man said, "actually I just heard about it."

"All right," said Socrates. "So you don't really know if it's true or not. Now let's try the second test, the test of Goodness. Is what you are about to tell me about my student something good?"

"No, on the contrary . . ."

"So," Socrates continued, "you want to tell me something bad about him even though you're not certain it's true?"

The man shrugged, a little embarrassed.

Socrates continued. "You may still pass though, because there is a third test—the filter of Usefulness. Is what you want to tell me about my student going to be useful to me?"

"No, not really."

"Well," concluded Socrates, "if what you want to tell me is neither True, nor Good, nor even Useful, why tell it to me at all?"

Whether or not this story is true, it seems to be somewhat in line with what philosophers call the Socratic method of questioning. The point, though, is quite clear. Why should you develop your opinions about anyone or anything in the world unless you can vouch for the accuracy of the facts? Being mindful of this is even more important in this age of mass media. You cannot put yourself in another person's shoes unless you have some direct access to the information regarding that person. Even then, you should be careful to ensure it is worth your effort to do so.

What Should You Know?

There is a fascinating parallel to this in the Sherlock Holmes stories written by Sir Arthur Conan Doyle. In *A Study in Scarlet*, Holmes tells Dr. Watson he was previously unaware that the Earth revolves around the sun. Moreover, now that he's learned it, he will do his best to forget it. When Watson protests, Holmes imperiously interrupts: "What the deuce is it to me? You say that we go round the sun. If we went round the moon it would not make a pennyworth of difference to me or to my work." Sherlock Holmes believes that the mind has a finite capacity for information storage, and learning *useless* things reduces one's ability to learn *useful* things.

Whether or not this is, in fact, true, it is a good lesson for all of us to bear in mind. We should strive to only take in pertinent knowledge, and even then to only occupy our minds with knowledge that is relevant to our lives. I must confess that I am a big trivia buff, and I relish "useless" knowledge on a daily basis. *But when it comes to evaluating other people and circumstances seriously, you would be wise to reserve judgment until stringent parameters are met.* This will help you form honest opinions of things instead of reacting to potentially incendiary gossip that will, inevitably, come your way. Such gossip is most usually intended to make you form an aggressive and negative opinion.

You may believe there is no way you could ever be swept up into the kind of mass hysteria that made so many Germans follow Hitler. However, do your best to imagine the German population's distorted point of view during the tumultuous 1930s and 1940s when they were pounded by Nazi propaganda through the newly formed mass media; this may give you a new sense of how those people were manipulated as the Nazis built an empire of evil, perhaps unique in all of human history. I have German friends, and I do not believe that all the German people in the thirties and forties were evil. I do, however, believe their government embraced the most basal animal instincts to dominate, and that most German citizens allowed their extremist politicians to take small steps that eventually led to dictatorship and eventual tragedy for everyone—*including* the German people.

Pigs or Lincolns?

We have all heard that ignorance is bliss. Whether or not this is true is another philosophic conundrum. When I was in college at the University of North Carolina at Asheville, my philosophy professor, a man named Dr. Deryl Howard, asked our class: "Would you rather be a happy pig or a depressed Abraham Lincoln?" In other words, would you rather be an ignorant but contented pig, or a knowledgeable Lincoln, weighed down by the cares of the Civil War? I thought about this for a long time, and decided I would rather be a happy pig. Maybe you feel the same way, but it doesn't matter. The truth is that you and I are not pigs. We may not be Lincolns, either, but we are certainly closer to him than we are to pigs. That is why we, as humans, are the creatures that control atomic bombs and fly ships into space.

We have been given, or obtained, in one way or another, power over many creatures, including pigs. We dominate much of Earth, so the way you feel and the impact you make on this planet is important to me and everyone else. I have heard that successful politicians such as Bill Clinton will stand before a large crowd and sometimes ignore the 99 percent who are supporters, focusing on the 1 percent of dissenters. Why train attention on the supporters—the majority—if you can spend your energy, instead, to possibly win over that 1 percent? This is another way of visualizing the power that negative people often command.

Do you realize that, in all of the six original Star Wars movies, the only being who is alive in every single film is Darth Vader? This is a testament to the significance of the dark side. In fact, you could therefore say the entire Star Wars saga is really about the dark side. Whatever the future of Star Wars may be in the hands of the Disney Corporation, its new owner, it is, at its honest core, the story of Darth Vader. Vader is portrayed as a talented young man, originally repressed by his society, who is sadly dragged through all the terrible qualities of humanity, both personally and politically. He is a child who, because of the gifts of his intellect and his unique relationship to the Force, is positioned by the Jedi as a candidate for salvation of the galaxy. And, once that salvation is granted due to good, synchronistic fortune, is thrust into a violent and exploitative world, full of confusing opportunities. It's very similar to the saga we see play out, again and again, with child celebrities. We can imagine Lucas is thinking of how our society treats up-and-coming talent, adoring and grooming them as kids until we eventually thrust them into the cutthroat world of show business.

Whatever your age as you read these words, you must absorb the lessons of Darth Vader. It may seem cool to don the shiny black helmet and flowing, raven cape and to wield the searing red lightsaber. The reality is that you do not want to be trapped behind that helmet, separated from life, and full of regret. Each day when you awaken, you want to breathe the air into your lungs, without it passing through some electronic system. You want to feel the world around you rather than merely sense it through robotic hands. You want to interact with the warm, organic elements around you each day.

The Death of Darth Vader

In the end, Darth Vader himself rejects his electronic mask. When he tells Luke to remove it, Luke says, "But you'll die!" But to Vader, it's worth death to look on his son with his own eyes. This is his final redemption from the dark side.

If you turn to the dark side—even slip there gradually—you might not end up in some dark, robotic suit, but you might as well. The movies are trying to tell you that this is what you will become. One way or another, you will end up separated from all the things you love. The sounds in your ears will be false representations of what is really there, and the words that come from your mouth will be crude mimics of what you are really trying to say and how you are trying to say it. Furthermore, you will end up just like Vader— a slave to some other power, as he was to the Emperor. It's kind of ironic that the powerful villain Vader was really just a puppet of the grotesque Emperor.

Who Is Your Emperor?

In the Star Wars movies, the Emperor was one person set on bringing Anakin to the dark side. However, in your own life, there may be many figures trying to do this. Most of them will probably not be as obvious as the Emperor. Stop and think, right now, about anyone you know who may represent the "Emperor figure." It could be a man or woman, young or old. It could be a family member, a friend, or a coworker. It could even be someone you really don't know in person—an individual you listen to on the radio or TV or Internet who makes an impact on how you think. Whatever the case, it will be a person who is constantly trying to convince you of *something*—a message intended to instill fear. It may not seem like a fear message at first, but when you think deeply about it, you will realize its real nature. The message will say if you don't do *this*, *that* will happen! In *Episode III: Revenge of the Sith*, it took less than 120 minutes for the Emperor to win over Anakin, but in real life, it can take weeks, months, or years.

Zero in on the forces in your life that might be trying to sway you to a defensive, fear-based mindset, and get rid of them immediately! Be smart, and understand now what is happening to you. The dark side of the Force is very powerful, but it will crumble when you have clear vision. If you have any doubt that your mind's relationship to these forces makes a huge impact on your reality, just look at what science has to tell you.

Chapter Thirteen

Grasp the Latest Science

"Don't be too proud of this technological terror you've constructed. The ability to destroy a planet is insignificant next to the power of the Force."

—Darth Vader to Admiral Motti, *Episode IV: A New Hope*

If you are like me, you are a lover of science. Fortunately, we live at a time when science has reinforced the concepts of the Force featured in this book. In fact, your spiritual identity and its relationship to the universe around you has been proven time and time again. It's good for you to understand this from a scientific point of view so you can better explain the Force to your inquisitive, and often skeptical, friends and family when needed. To fully comprehend the scientific angle, perhaps the best place to start is with what physicists call the double-slit experiment.

The Double-Slit Experiment

The basic double-slit experiment was first conducted in the early 1800s by an English scientist named Thomas Young. Therefore, it is also called Young's Experiment. His original intention was to simply determine if light behaves as a particle or a wave. He thought by shining a light through slits, he could determine the physical property of light by seeing how it passed through the slits.

Today, scientists take a piece of material with two narrow slits cut into it side by side, and shine a laser at those slits. They analyze the pattern the laser light makes when it comes out on the other side. If light behaves as a wave, one pattern should be produced. If light behaves as particles, it should create a different pattern. Over the years, this experiment has been done with various particles, but again and again, the results have blown the minds of scientists.

Electrons are extremely tiny pieces of subatomic matter. When individual electrons were fired, one at a time, like bullets from a single gun, toward the slits, the pattern indicated a wave formation, as if many electrons were being fired at once. Scientists could not understand this, so they installed measuring devices to see which slit(s) electrons were passing through. When they did this, the electrons behaved as particles again. Huh?

What the experimenters determined was that the particles change their behavior based upon how they are *observed*. When you are not observing something, it exists as a multitude of potential probabilities. But when you observe something, your observation dramatically affects how that thing snaps into a particular position or reality. I know this sounds incredible, yet physicists have the math to prove it. If you really want to understand the double-slit experiment better, then do an Internet search for the phrase and you'll find some great demonstrations, such as the "Dr. Quantum" animation featured in the 2006 movie *What the Bleep!?: Down the Rabbit Hole.*

In *Episode IV: A New Hope*, the success of the rebellion hinges on Luke Skywalker, barreling toward the Death Star in his X-wing starfighter. He has to land one perfect shot in the vulnerable exhaust port of the massive, sinister space station. The pressure could not be greater with Darth Vader right on his tail, and yet Luke shocks everyone when he makes a critical decision. He hears the wise, haunting words of Obi-Wan in his mind: "Use the Force, Luke. Let go." Luke confidently puts away his targeting computer, a small screen at eye level, designed to guide him on his course.

"Luke," calls a slightly panicked voice from the control room radio, "you switched off your targeting computer. What's wrong?"

"Nothing," he replies. "I'm all right." Guided only by the Force, Luke fires, sending his blasts dead-on to the target, blowing the Death Star to smithereens. We can compare this scenario to the lessons of the double-slit experiments.

Before Luke fired, the destination of his blasts existed in a state of multiple probabilities. However, when he connected his calm, trained mind to the possibilities, he was able to select one singular outcome. Of all the things that could have happened, his consciousness was refined enough to focus it on what he wanted to experience. In this case, the blasts were the particles, and Luke was the observer, engaging those particles and making them behave as he wished, focusing them into the exhaust port, similar to controlling the way electrons might pass through the double slits.

Spooky Action at a Distance

In fact, the mind's ability to directly affect matter in the universe seems to transcend even the apparent limits of space and time. This is due to a phenomenon scientists call *nonlocality*. It is so strange that Albert Einstein called it "spooky action at a distance." It appears that the action of a particular particle can instantaneously affect the action of another particular particle, no matter how separated they may be by space. We know that light travels at 186,000 miles per second. Therefore, regardless of how quickly an effect travels through space, we generally presume it will require some time to travel from point A to point B. In fact, we define a light year as the distance light travels, in a vacuum, in one Julian year (365.25 days). So if even light takes some time to travel, however quickly, how can two particles directly and *instantaneously* affect each other regardless of distance? It is due to a mysterious property physicists call *quantum entanglement*.

Physics defines quantum entanglement as *a physical phenomenon that occurs when pairs or groups of particles are generated or interact in ways such that the quantum state of each particle cannot be described independently—instead, a quantum state may be given for the system as a whole.* In layman's terms, it is one particle seeming to affect another without any time delay. The idea of this relationship between two particles is thrilling and mind-boggling, but what makes all of this even more exciting is an experiment recently conducted in Canada.

In 2014, some groundbreaking experiments were done by physicists at the Institute for Quantum Computing (IQC) at the University of Waterloo in Ontario. They were able to achieve quantum entanglement between more than two particles. The scientists got three particles to entangle, all instantly affecting each other, and opening the door to the world of *multi-party* quantum entanglement. This is sensational on at least two levels. Firstly, imagine the ability to technologically exchange information immediately between various points. This is groundwork for the Internet of the future. Currently, the Internet can allow millions of people around the globe, and even in space for that matter, to all access the same content on a webpage and even interact through it. However, it does not happen without delay, and the electronic "pipelines" are frequently clogged, causing buffering problems. The findings at the University of Waterloo could create a new groundwork for multiple points to experience the same information at the same moment, without relying on crude conductors, which impede the flow. But it is the second implication that is really astounding.

What the IQC experiments have truly shown is a property of how the universe works. We now have some objective evidence that the known universe is indeed homogenous on some level, meaning that all points are universally connected. We can predict that our galaxy is full of entangled points. It reminds me of how black hole science slowly developed. The first time the term "black hole" was used in print was in 1964 by journalist Ann Ewing. At that time, it was still a subject of debate, primarily considered in the realm of science fiction by the general public. We now know the core of our very own Milky Way galaxy contains a supermassive black hole. In fact, many cosmologists think black holes may exist in every known galaxy. Our grasp of the universe, in general, is changing in astounding ways. In the 1990s, scientists believed there were no more than nine planets. Now we know there are more than 1,000 planets here in our own galaxy. George Lucas's vision of the universe may be closer to reality than we think. The more we discover, the more we see beyond the components of the universe and into the way in which it is assembled. We are learning, every day, that there is not only much more here, but that all is constantly interacting in ways relegated only to fantasy before.

Modern science brings a new clarity to how the Jedi can be mentally in touch with events and people across the entire universe. When a Jedi feels a disturbance or presence in the Force, it is because her mind is sensitive to the bonds of entanglement that spread infinitely in all directions. And, just as a Jedi can receive information from those connections, she can also transmit will-power back into those connections, influencing how everything else behaves.

It might be easy to accept all these peculiarities of quantum physics and still doubt they can make a realistic impact on our macroscopic world and lives. However, you must consider two important factors. First, what is your brain, but a conglomeration of atoms, filled with subatomic particles, constantly firing and forming your own self-aware consciousness? Anything possible in the quantum world must also be possible within you, because you are ultimately constructed of those same quantum particles. The second factor leads us to another great experimental finding.

The Quantum World Is Your World

Between 1996 and 2003, four Nobel Prizes were given for work related to macroscopic quantum phenomena. One of my favorite examples of experimentation in this realm was published by *Nature* in 2010. The title was "Scientists Supersize Quantum Mechanics: Largest Ever Object Put into Quantum State." Scientists at the University of California, Santa Barbara, constructed a tiny "paddle," only 30 micrometres long. That is larger than some human hairs, and thus very much a part of our realistic daily lives. The lead scientist, Andrew Cleland, and his team cooled the paddle to make it more sensitive to quantum forces, and less sensitive to disruptive outside forces. At that point, they were able to place the paddle in the state in which it was both vibrating *and* standing still at the same time. Yes, that's right: Moving and standing still at once. This is similar to what physicists call a *cat state*, based on a classic thought experiment called Schrödinger's cat (named for the German physicist Erwin Schrödinger).

Schrödinger's Cat

In Schrödinger's thought experiment, a cat is placed in a sealed box that also contains a vial of poison. At some undetermined point, the vial will open, killing the cat. But since we can't know without opening the box whether the vial has opened, as long as the box remains sealed, the cat is both dead and not dead.

The cat state is one in which two diametrically opposed conditions occur at the same time. In 2005, a team from Maryland's

National Institute of Standards and Technology (NIST) was able to make six atoms spin together in two *opposite* directions at the same time. You don't have to comprehend how such things are logically possible in order to appreciate how wondrous the proven work of these scientists has become. The point is that all the seeming madness and magic of the quantum world also exists right here, in this macro realm in which you live. However improbable, anything is possible. The world seems to be a flexible medium in which opposites can coexist, as well as all variables in between. You, as a part of this world, are intimately, intrinsically, and immediately connected to all those variables.

A Holographic Universe

Given all this, how do we best classify the makeup of reality? Many physicists think it can be accurately called a *holographic universe*. What does that mean?

First, let's look at the basic building blocks of the mind-body-environment relationship. Not surprisingly, the Internet is a good model for reality. It's more of a shadow of reality. You could even say the Internet exemplifies technology imitating life. In my paranormal work, people often ask me questions like, "Where is the spiritual realm?" This question is not truly suited to the issue. It's kind of like asking, "What temperature is this sound?" The two issues are not related. The spiritual realm, just like the Internet, is a stream of flowing information.

If you bring up a webpage and see a tree, you know that a real tree is not actually there. What you are seeing are patterns of information organized in a way to represent a tree. No matter how stunning and detailed it may seem, it is still light hitting your eyes from a screen. You are witnessing the temporary organization of a stream of information. You might print out a two-dimensional, physical representation of that information, but a tree and a picture of a tree are still different things. If you tear up the paper, it does not take the tree off the screen. This is similar to the relationship between your body and spirit. Your spirit is the tree on the screen, and your body is the printout. This, in a nutshell, exemplifies the relationship between matter (your body) and energy (your body). Now let's stretch this into a three-dimensional context.

Flatland

The Star Wars movies are full of holographic imagery. Less than thirty minutes into the original film, we have the famous Princess Leia hologram pleading, "Help me, Obi-Wan Kenobi. You're my only hope." The very first time we glimpse Emperor Palpatine, he is a frightening hologram in the chamber of Darth Vader. Holograms, such as that of Admiral Ackbar, appear in war strategy rooms, as well. These typical holographic forms are presented in 3D, since we visualize the forms around us in three dimensions. However, many physicists and cosmologists believe there are more than three dimensions. Time is the fourth dimension, but mathematics and physics theory currently support ten or more. How can you possibly begin to comprehend what that actually means?

The best way to get some handle on the subject is to imagine yourself looking down on "lower" dimensions. This thought-provoking premise was developed by Edwin Abbot, an English schoolmaster and theologian. In 1884 he published a novella called *Flatland*. Imagine what would happen, he asked, if a world composed of two-dimensional beings had a brush with a three-dimensional being, such as yourself.

Just to refresh, the three dimensions are length, width, and height. You could also say they are back-and-forth, side-to-side, and up-and-down. Envision, if you can, looking down on a world that is completely flat and two-dimensional. From your point of view, it would look like a flat piece of paper. You might see the people as little circles. Inside a roofless home, they might seem to be moving around within a square border. (Keep in mind that to a Flatlander, the inside of the house would be hidden from sight.) If you were to single out a Flatlander and speak to him from above, all he would hear would be a disembodied voice. If you descended down into Flatland to visit him, he would see a line that appeared out of nowhere, like a ghost materializing. The length of the line would constantly change as you moved up and down through his dimension. If you swept down and carried him up into the sky, his world would be a temporary blur of scary and wild sensations as he floated back down. How could he possibly describe that "mystical" experience to his peers? All of this is beautifully illustrated by Carl Sagan in an episode of the TV series *Cosmos: A Personal Voyage*. You can find a clip on the net by searching for "Carl Sagan" and "Flatland."

After thinking about how a person living in a two-dimensional world would perceive a visitor from a three-dimensional world, you should be able to imagine how confused we, as three-dimensional creatures, would feel when faced with phenomena from other dimensions. I find it ironic that scientists, who pride themselves on skeptical thinking, are often too close-minded and unimaginative to consider how we would experience such phenomena. It's also important to emphasize that "skeptic" is one of the most misused terms in the vocabulary. It should denote one who wisely reserves judgment without all proper evidence yet to judge, instead of one who actively dismisses.

The important thing to remember is that *those who are making true, practical headway in technology are those who embrace new and unfamiliar paradigms of data.* After all, if we knew everything, science would come to an end. There would be nothing to discover. As it turns out, despite our fantastic headway, we are just learning how complex, beautiful, and wonderful our universe is. To grasp that you live in a holographic universe is to grasp that you are in a multilayered, interconnected reality, and that what you experience on the surface is just a representation of the vast, expansive forces that lie beneath. *You, yourself, are a mentally active holographic representation, and so you are capable of impacting all those other holographic representations around you, no matter how bizarre, far away, inaccessible, or unobtainable they may seem.*

Over the centuries, many enlightened teachers have sensed all this, but the true scientists—those who actually achieve practical progress—are doing so by properly applying tools that can help us humans interface with all these dimensions spanning the universe.

I should point out that it is a mistake to rely solely on tools of scientific investigation and apply some godlike authority to them. All human tools, no matter how advanced, were envisioned by humans, constructed by humans, calibrated by humans, used by humans, and interpreted by humans. It is impossible to remove the subjective component from science, and all data can be swayed, intentionally or unintentionally, to produce skewed results. That said, tools are the things that have allowed us to rocket beyond other creatures, and tools help us live better, more enjoyable lives each day. In Star Wars, the ultimate tool of the Jedi is the lightsaber, and it is one of the strangest and most enigmatic instruments ever imagined.

Jedi Tools

In *Episode IV: A New Hope*, Obi-Wan Kenobi tells Luke, during their first meeting, "I have something for you. Your father wanted you to have this when you were old enough . . . your father's lightsaber. This is the weapon of a Jedi Knight—not as clumsy or random as a blaster; an elegant weapon for a more civilized age." Before we get into the technical aspects of what lightsabers represent, it's important to think of their colors as storytelling devices.

The most intimidating villains in Star Wars—Darth Vader, Darth Maul, and Count Dooku—all use red lightsabers. This is extremely significant. If we look at the spectrum of visible colors, red is at the lowest frequency (the frequency one step lower, outside of visible range, is infrared). Frequency is a measurement of how much a thing pulsates, and vibration is the core of life. Absence of vibration is death. These characters, who dish out death unapologetically, bear lightsabers that function at the lowest frequency we can see with our eyes—the same red color that indicates it's dangerous to proceed at traffic lights. They are also cloaked in black, which represents the absence of anything, including vibration and life. We see these same colors distinctly depicted in nature on creatures such as the deadly black widow spider and some venomous coral snakes. Yoda's lightsaber is green, a color associated with lush growth, prosperity, and a traffic light signaling us that it is okay and safe to proceed.

The Power of a Lightsaber

A Jedi usually has his lightsaber nearby. It can certainly be used for many purposes, aside from fighting. In *The Empire Strikes Back*, when Han Solo discovers Luke unconscious with hypothermia on snowy Hoth, he uses Luke's lightsaber to cut open a tauntaun that has just died. Han uses the creature's hot, slimy guts to provide lifesaving warmth for Luke. In *The Phantom Menace*, Qui-Gon Jinn uses his lightsaber to cut through a blast door, easily turning its almost impenetrable material into molten metal. Time and time again, a Jedi relies on his lightsaber. When he loses it in an action scene, the Force can bring it swiftly back to his hand.

It is fascinating to see that characters who enjoy such mystical powers over matter still rely on tools. The lightsaber, the most significant tool, has a very special, personalized relationship with the Jedi. In fact, the lightsaber almost seems like an extension of the Jedi, enhancing his ability to use the Force. In the real world, you will rarely be in need of an energy blade to engage in duels; there are actually other tools that can help you more effectively transmit your intentions through the Force. They are within the mysterious realm of what many call radionics.

Radionics

Despite all our technological achievements, we still do not understand the exact nature of consciousness. Therefore, anything associated with consciousness is equally mysterious and controversial. That said, I will give you my personal experience with a type of device often called radionics "wishing machines." Early versions of these devices were created around 100 years ago during the heyday of medical quackery. The value of the device was obscured by a confusing wave of fraudulent machines. However, as years passed, private researchers continued doing experiments with the wishing machine and came to believe these boxes could be used to enhance the mind-body-environment relationship. I first bought one around the year 2000 from a reclusive engineer in California. It cost me $300, though many of these machines sell for thousands.

What I received was a wooden box with nine knobs (like potentiometers or volume knobs) that could each adjust from 0 to 10. There were also two plates—an input plate, which was metal, and an output plate, which was plastic. To operate it, you represent what you want to achieve (your wish) and then follow some simple instructions to tune the box, so that your intention is transmitted through the output plate into the universe. At that point, you put the box away and allow it to work for you as you go about your normal daily business.

Since I had paid $300 for the box, my first wish was to get my $300 back. I set up the box for this, and less than forty-eight hours later I received a phone call from a major hotel saying they had a group that wanted someone to tell local legends for an hour, and they would pay $300. I found it thought-provoking, to say the least, that this was the exact amount for which I'd wished. It seemed as if, via synchronicity, my wish had come true. From there, I continued to experiment with these devices. I had such tremendous success that I created a special project.

I found a man in South Carolina who is the very best at making these weird wishing machines. We created the Wishing Machine Project, making these boxes available for people to experiment with all over the world. The feedback was astonishing. Thousands of letters of appreciation came back from people who had achieved positive results regarding wealth, health, happiness, and virtually any kind of scenario you can imagine (within the natural laws of the universe). We started publishing many of these testimonials, and you can see and hear them at my site *www.WishingMachineProject.com*. The site also has some videos explaining how we think the machines work. The feedback coming in from people in all cultures is being used to constantly create new models and updated devices. This gives us some clues into the future of conscious-sensitive technologies.

When the Wright brothers invented the airplane in 1903, much of the scientific establishment thought the creation of a reliable, heavier-than-air flying craft was impossible. Editors of the prestigious journal *Scientific American* said they doubted the "alleged experiments" and, citing how little the Wright brothers were taken seriously by the press of the time, asked how U.S. newspapers, "alert as they are, allowed these sensational performances to escape their notice." When Thomas Edison invented the phonograph, the first machine to record and play back sound, many people believed it was a hoax. After all, *everybody knew you couldn't record a* sound—*an intangible thing!* When he demonstrated the phonograph for crowds, he was often questioned as to whether or not it was a magic trick (with hidden sound tubes) or a ventriloquist act. At that time, the average human mind could not comprehend how a sound could be "captured" and replayed. At this point in history, we may not be able to fully comprehend how a machine can record and enhance human consciousness, but this could be what wishing machines and similar future technologies will do.

The Need for Focus

Work with the Force requires great mindfulness, as well as some focus every day on what you want. When you send out your desire, it is the sympathetic resonance that activates corresponding energies in the universe. It may be that "mind machines" such as those in radionics operate by a principle I've termed *automated sympathetic resonance*, or ASR. The idea is that once you place your intention into a wishing machine, it continues sending out that intention even when you are distracted by other things in real time. It might be kind of like comparing a paper map to a GPS unit. When you're driving toward a destination, you can refer to an old-fashioned map, but that means you must pay more attention to it, looking at it from time to time and staying aware of upcoming turns. However, a GPS unit allows you to go ahead and program the entire trip. Then you can just kick back and, so long as the GPS unit operates correctly, enjoy the ride, taking guidance from the computer when needed.

New Tools of the Future

The new era of technology is taking us more and more toward consciousness-sensitive instruments and media that will astound us. That means these devices will also be able to interact with the Force, acting as an extension and conductor of you. Eventually, this will blur the line between the organic and inorganic, man and machine. If you look at a human under a microscope, you will find iron, copper, sulfur, tin, silicon, and many other substances also strewn throughout the "inanimate" universe. This shows us, in a very real way, that we humans are not separated from the universe—we just sometimes feel we are due to our egocentric attitudes. You are a part of everything that exists around you, and the new generation of mind-powered tools will help you make that connection to the Force throughout the universe more powerfully than ever. In fact, you could say that wishing machine technology ultimately equals *Force machine* technology.

Many people consider the Star Wars movies works of science fiction. There is definitely plenty of technical eye candy to think about from an engineer's perspective. However, early on in *Episode IV: A New Hope*, Imperial Admiral Motti unwisely criticizes Darth Vader for his trust in the Force: "Don't try to frighten us with your sorcerer's ways, Lord Vader. Your sad devotion to that ancient religion has not helped you conjure up the stolen data tapes, or given you clairvoyance enough to find the Rebels' hidden fortress." Vader seizes Motti in the infamous Force chokehold. It is interesting that in this scene, early on in our introduction to the Force, it is referred to as a "religion." This sets a fascinating tone for the rest of the series, combining a world full of technological achievement with a spiritual power that can ultimately overcome technology.

The Material and the Spiritual

We frequently make the mistake of feeling a scientific view of the world cannot coexist with a spiritual view. However, to feel this way does not realistically acknowledge all of the experiences of human life. Charles Darwin, the father of evolutionary biology, had a degree in theology from Christ's College, Cambridge. Historians say his interest in religion and the spiritual landscape of life inspired his biological pursuits. It is ironic that the image of a man who valued so many different views of the world in proper context, has often been hijacked by strict materialists. Galileo was imprisoned by the Roman Catholic Church in 1616 for his heretical opinions, based on his findings as an astronomer that the Earth is not the center of the universe. Yet today, the Catholic Church operates the Vatican Observatory in Castel Gandolfo, Italy.

Science is an imperfect system that is intended to perpetually correct itself. Religion tries to enhance human spirituality through imperfect human management. The two are different perspectives, and yet they occupy the same universe; there is a level at which the two must intersect and, for that matter, overlay. We're always struggling to find that connection, and we will surely get better. But to do so requires our willingness to honestly acknowledge the benefits and flaws of both science and religion and to help bring balance to the important roles they can both play in human life.

The purpose of using the Force for good is to ensure our whole world becomes a better place. Some of the world's brightest scientists, such as Dr. Michio Kaku, professor of Theoretical Physics at the City College of New York, often talk about the work of a Soviet astronomer named Nikolai Kardashev. In 1964, he proposed a scale, now known as the Kardashev Scale, to hypothetically describe the progress of a planet's people. Civilizations, he argued, can be divided into three types. A Type I civilization uses all available resources impinging on its home planet, a Type II harnesses all the energy of its star (in our case, the sun), and a Type III of its galaxy. Here's how that would play out.

The March of Civilization

Right now, Earth is a Type 0 civilization. That is because we live on a planet booming and teeming with power sources, high above us and deep below us and all around us, yet we still have not learned to harmoniously tap into all this power. Let's say our work with fossil fuels, solar power, windmills, hydroelectric, geothermal, electrostatic, and other (even yet-to-be-discovered) technologies eventually combines so that we feel we are making the most efficient use possible of everything Earth has to offer. Presumably at that point we would know enough to power ships that would allow us to do the same with our sun, channeling its nuclear reactions into beneficial resources. We would branch out beyond the sun, bouncing from system to system, taking what is needed. Imagine this: we get a whole new insight on "alien space travel," whether or not we on Earth have indeed been occasionally visited by exploratory probes or representatives of Type II or Type III civilizations. Theoretically, once beings start traveling outside of their own galaxies we can think of them as Type IV. Dr. Michio Kaku has suggested that our human civilization on Earth may attain Type I status in 100–200 years, Type II status in a few thousand years, and Type III status in 100,000 to a million years. What a fascinating way of envisioning the future of humans, should we make it through manmade and natural extinction-level disasters.

Because we are egocentric creatures, when we think of the future we usually envision being able to zoom in spaceships from planet to planet in a few hours or days, ride in a flying car, or wield blasters and lightsabers. Yet, perhaps the most thought-provoking line in the Star Wars series is the famous opening of every movie: *A long time ago, in a galaxy far, far away* . . .

That opening line reverses your usual way of thinking and suddenly opens your mind to cosmic cycles of time so great that concepts of technological past and future become almost irrelevant. We humans on Earth are just the new kids on the block. The Star Wars saga might be a cautionary tale from the past about how things can (and probably will) always go wrong at times. You can change the surface of technology, but the people underneath are attached to the same motivations and spiritual needs.

The fact that the story the movies tell happened a long time ago in a different part of the universe implies that there is something cogent, consistent, and cohesive about how life exists and perceives its own "living experience" all across the universe. However, the pendulum always swings back and forth, from periods of greed and power-hungry dictatorship, to eras of hope and enlightenment. If anything, Star Wars is the story of how this balance perpetually alternates as civilizations expand and collapse, regardless of their position in space or time.

Star Wars takes place in a Type II civilization, in which the characters travel about the galaxy conducting business the way we currently travel around the earth. When you think about this in terms of the Kardashev Scale, the stories and scenes become even more interesting. Droids and landspeeders—things that we humans now dream of—have become old, rusted parts lying in a junk heap on Tatooine in some fantastic future. What is stressed in the films is that scientific and technological development will always continue, but, at the end of the day, the richness of the living experience comes down to an individual's relationship with the Force.

The Wormhole Brain

In *The Secret Wisdom of Kukulkan*, I explored what it means to be a human connected to the universe. If I were to take a great hand and squeeze every bit of empty space and water from your body, what was left over would be the size of a pea. How is it that this amount of matter is *all* we can see of what holds *all* your personal memories, experiences, hopes, aspirations, desires, and personality? Furthermore, that ball of physical matter is constantly changing into a new form—we call the process aging. However, as you've no doubt heard, most of the cells in your body are constantly being replaced with new cells. Parts of your intestines are only two or three days old. Your taste buds are ten days old. Your skin is between two and four weeks old. So, really, what are you? The closest we can get to answering this is what I call the Wormhole Brain Theory.

Wormhole Brain Theory

A wormhole is a tunnel in space-time connecting two different points. It is most often brought up in discussions about time travel. A large wormhole might allow you to move from the past to the future, and vice versa. But wormholes are about more than simply allowing time travel; they allow *information flow*. If we were to condense most of the philosophies about the brain and consciousness, it seems plausible that each person's consciousness is a tiny wormhole, a wormhole brain. This means your body is sort of like a physical computer, but your wormhole brain connects that computer to the "cloud," a vaster, separate place where information is stored en masse. This might explain some telepathic and other so-called psychic phenomena in which people seem to have shared experiences in the cloud. It could also apply to dreaming and why certain genes act like specialized antennas, connecting with signals from the cloud for particular talents, gifts, proclivities, and diseases. Of course, your relationship with the Force may determine how mentally accessible cloud information is at any given time. At first, it might seem like too great a leap to conceive of a place where your consciousness and those of everyone else are stored. However, it's really not much of a stretch at all.

Dark Matter

When Sir Isaac Newton published his work *Philosophiæ Naturalis Principia Mathematica* (Latin for "Mathematical Principles of Natural Philosophy," often referred to simply as the *Principia*) in

1687, the world changed. The book laid the groundwork for physics and classical mechanics, with astounding insight into gravity and optics. For hundreds of years, it was almost the sole authority for understanding how bodies behaved both on earth and in space. To this day Newtonian physics, as presented in the seventeenth century, is still perfectly suited to calculate many complex scenarios accurately. However, in the twentieth century, as physics advanced, we realized that Newton's worldview was too limited to explain what happens, especially on the subatomic level. On the macrolevel, too, astronomers realized something was wrong.

In a nutshell, based on Newton's calculations alone, there is simply not enough matter in the known universe to keep it all together and spinning in the nice, organized patterns we observe. Struggling to explain this problem, some scientists, such as Dutch astronomer Jan Oort and Swiss astronomer Fritz Zwicky, started speculating in the 1930s about the existence of "dark matter" and "dark energy." Since we couldn't see enough stuff out there to explain the gravitational dynamics of the galaxy, they said, there must be something there that we can't see. Since then, most mainstream scientists have embraced this mysterious phenomenon enthusiastically.

Let me stress how weird this all is. Scientists, who are devoted to finding empirical evidence for phenomena, say there is a substance in our galaxy that is defined by the very fact we cannot directly detect it! According to the scientists, dark matter cannot be seen directly with telescopes; evidently it neither emits nor absorbs light or other electromagnetic radiation at any significant level. It is otherwise hypothesized to simply be matter that is not reactant to light. Instead, the existence and properties of dark matter are inferred from its gravitational effects on visible matter, radiation, and the large-scale structure of the universe.

Fair enough. Let us pause to admire the fact that some of the most esteemed scientists in the world, with access to the best budgets and research tools, are assuring us that everything we can see out there is a glittering foam on the surface of a mysterious black ocean. Just how big is this ocean of the unknown? Here's the real kicker: Scientists believe that dark matter makes up 84.5 percent of the total matter in the universe. Dark energy, a hypothesized unknown form of energy, plus dark matter together make up 95.1 percent of the total content of the universe.

The world's very smartest people—most accomplished scientists—are looking out there into the universe as deeply as they can every day—and they are telling us that 95.1 percent of what they *know* is there, is not explainable. This means that we still don't know what the heck is going on in this universe. On one hand, this may seem frightening. On the other hand, it is a wondrous thing; it frees your mind to explore all the possibilities for yourself, making the most of your limited lifespan.

Some authors and researchers these days, like Dr. Rebecca Hardcastle, talk about "exoconsciousness." There are a lot of different views on what this term currently means, but to me it means that what you believe is your internal consciousness is actually connected to a collective consciousness outside yourself. Maybe dark matter and dark energy hide the pathways and circuit boards where the connections are made.

UFO enthusiasts have long talked about craft that appear to be almost organic, shifting shape and color to match their surrounding elements. We have stories about alien beings that appear seamlessly connected to the panels of their ships, controlling them with thought alone. It may be that as we better understand our relationship with the universe, through the Force we will create consciousness-sensitive machines that allow us to overcome the current boundaries of traveling through space, and even time. Perhaps if there exist beings in a Type V civilization, the conscious minds of its populace are so connected with the universe that they don't need machines at all. Just as a Jedi can spring far into the air, what if Type V beings can fly like Superman, and even teleport through dimensions? They would certainly appear as godlike beings to us humans. Fanciful or not, this is another way of imagining just how far the human mind and spirit might be capable of taking us, if only we can properly follow the Force.

Science and Spirituality

Remember that in Star Wars, the Jedi are not hermit-monks who give up creature comforts for the natural world. On the contrary, they are very much in tune with the benefits of technology. Most of the Jedi are expert pilots. They use communication devices and function very smoothly in their manmade environments. In other words, you do not have to choose a spiritually oriented life over a scientifically oriented one, or vice versa. You should, in fact, strive for that perfect balance. Doing so means *you must clearly understand the difference between science and spirituality, respecting both.*

The word "science" is often misused. People will say things like "science tells us this" or "according to science." This makes science sound like some authoritative figure handing down an unflinching verdict. In fact, *science is a method of exploration, and nothing more.* It is much more appropriate to say "scientific research indicates" or "according to the scientific approach." When used properly, science can help unlock the most powerful secrets in the universe. But when used improperly, it can sow enormous destruction and unimaginable pain. In his 1981 book, *The Mismeasure of Man*, the late Stephen Jay Gould cites how often "scientists," especially in the nineteenth century, claimed there was a biological reason for racism, sexism, and social classes by measuring human craniums and grossly skewing psychological and physical data. This demonstrates some of the weaknesses of the scientific method, and how much there still remains to learn.

Even today there are many issues that confound modern scientists. When scientists conduct medical experiments, handing subjects a combination of new drugs alongside sugar pills, they cannot figure out why the sugar pills sometimes work just as well as the drugs. Scientists call this the *placebo effect* and consider it an unexplained phenomenon. But there is a reason the placebo effect works. It is because the mind alone can achieve astounding results we cannot yet scientifically understand. These are just some of the weaknesses of science.

The scientific method itself entails observation, recording of observations, analysis of possible cause and effect, and then the testing of hypotheses. Eventually out of this, science constructs a theory, which is subject to further tests through observation and experimentation. Scientific information is only as valuable as the methodology of the scientist.

In medieval times, many people didn't believe in meteorites since it seemed obvious that rocks can't fall from the sky. Who could have proven how many rocks are really floating around out there? Humans never saw an actual, full photo of Earth's globe from space until 1972! This demonstrates how early we still are in our scientific explorations.

The Basis of Spirituality

If not scientifically based, what is spirituality? Spirituality is something each person must define for himself or herself. For me, it is the quest for peace, harmony, and joy in my universe. And so, you might ask, am I at peace with the universe in harmony and joy? This moment, I am. And each moment I am responsible for keeping it that way. Spirituality is much simpler and more instinctual than science. At first, spiritual studies seem to deal with less obvious phenomena than science. Yet, the spiritual quest—*one's full realization of this enigmatic energy called life*—should, to us, as living beings, be the most obvious thing of all. You might need to turn this over in your mind a few times, but spirituality is the ultimate quest to understand all aspects of the Force.

In *Episode III: Revenge of the Sith,* when Anakin is almost burned to death, the Emperor uses scientific technology to save his life, encasing Anakin's body in a powerful, inorganic suit. From then on, Darth Vader is essentially a brain in a jar—albeit the most impressive jar in the galaxy. For years, Vader dominates the Empire with his artificial body, inflicting pain and fear wherever he goes. But, in *Episode VI: Return of the Jedi*, after he throws the Emperor down a chasm and finally lies crumpled and defeated beside his son, he says something extremely revealing. "Luke, help me take this mask off."

"But you'll die," responds his concerned son.

"Nothing can stop that now," says Vader. "Just for once . . . let me look on you with my own eyes."

That scene exemplifies the relationship between the ultimate value of the human experience and the sad gap that seeing the world via technology alone can create. Lucas wants to teach us about the balance between those two aspects. The good news is that we, as enlightened humans in the real world, have the opportunity to understand this.

The scientific establishment and those who stress spiritual lessons are not at odds. This is proven each time experiments are done, like the double-slit experiments, which emphasize the tangible impact you, *personally*, as a spiritual being, have on reality. You, as the observer, are also creating what is observed.

The Power of Observation

I have always been impressed by Albert Einstein's famous quote, "Reality is merely an illusion, albeit a very persistent one." What exactly did he mean by that? You could say, at the very least, he meant that different beings perceive a different reality. At this moment, what you see, hear, and smell is surely quite different from what a fly would perceive at your same location. It would be even more different for a microorganism on a nearby tabletop, or an eagle soaring overhead and peering down, to see the same thing you're seeing.

You might also say that Einstein was referring to changing optical perspective, given all his work with light. For example, if I hold a pencil up in front of my face, it looks as tall as a tree. If I place that pencil far away, it looks as tiny as a hairpin. Of course, I might hold a ruler next to the pencil to measure its length scientifically. However, if I move the pencil away with the ruler beside it, the inches marked on the ruler appear to shrink, as well.

I think Einstein meant all of that, and much more.

We can look farther away and deeper into the universe than ever, only to realize there is more and more we cannot explain. We can look closer and closer at the tiniest details of atoms, only to realize the smallest particles seem to pop in and out of this realm, as if they're constantly crackling between here and some other place. There are black holes everywhere, and we have no idea what is on the other end. Dark matter and energy engulf us, almost entirely. Ironically, science is giving us more evidence of magic and mystery than ever before, and you are the magician.

Remember, the universe is just that: "uni." It is one. Despite how we try to divide it all up, shake it around, and filter it through screens, we are always left with a single thing: For every action there is an equal and opposite reaction. In that simple and profound way, science and spirituality are one.

Chapter Fourteen

Your New Life

"The Force will be with you . . . always."

—Obi-Wan to Luke, *Episode IV: A New Hope*

Think about those words: "The Force will be with you . . . always." Pause and let them sink in for a bit—especially that word *always*. You exist right now, and you will always exist in some form. Maybe you will exist as a random spread of matter, like smoke drifting from a burning cigar. Perhaps you will be a star, blazing in some faraway galaxy. Maybe you'll be in a silent blade of grass or a molecule of water undulating on the sea. But for right now, this very moment, you are here, in this form. The decisions you make this very second will shift you toward your next phase, tomorrow and forever. What and where do you want to be? You have the control.

One of my favorite authors is Thomas Wolfe. He was from Asheville, North Carolina, my hometown, and lived from 1900 to 1938. Wolfe's most famous book was the literary classic, *Look Homeward, Angel*. It's a thick, autobiographical novel. When he was eighteen, Thomas Wolfe was at the bedside of his sick twenty-six-year-old brother, Ben. Thomas Wolfe wrote about watching his brother die of influenza. It is, in my opinion, one of the most touching, and vividly written parts of the book. I was especially struck by this sentence, as Wolfe reflects on what has happened to his dead, beloved brother: "We can believe in the nothingness of life, we can believe in the nothingness of death and of life after death—but who can believe in the nothingness of Ben?"

You are a being of infinite reach and power. Even death did not stop the spirit of Obi-Wan from coming back to mentor Luke. At the end of *Episode VI: Return of the Jedi*, we see the spirits of Obi-Wan, Yoda, and Anakin at the final celebration of victory over the Empire. Whether or not we take these depictions of Force ghosts literally or figuratively, they play a key role in the Star Wars saga for a reason. They are intended to drive home that your life is more than just where you are at this moment. You want to make the right decisions to continue enriching your experience for all time.

Steps to Using the Force

In order to live your new life as a Jedi, able to command your reality through the Law of Attraction, let's recap some of the basic steps you must take.

Prepare Your Mind

This means clearing your mind of negative baggage. You can only build a strong, lasting structure upon a stable foundation. No matter how impressive any progress you make might seem, it will eventually collapse—probably sooner than later—if you do not begin properly.

One of the key components, especially during this stage, is staying away from things that make you feel bad—particularly friends or family who continually pursue you with negative thoughts. Be mindful that energy flows where attention goes, and use that to empower only those things around you that will contribute to the strong, positive structure you are building. You might even use this knowledge to manifest the old Jedi mind trick.

You must also take time to sincerely forgive yourself for your past mistakes, and anyone else who has caused you pain. The past is gone, and so holding onto what happened, however bad it may have been at the time, can serve you no positive purpose now. Forgiving others is about helping yourself; it has nothing to do with them. Eventually, justice will be done in all situations.

Be Grateful

When you project a sincere feeling of gratitude for whatever you have for which to be thankful (no matter how small it may seem), you project a signal into the universe that reflects back even *more* things for which you will be grateful. This will quickly snowball until your life is absolutely brimming with wonderful things. You should awaken each day and remind yourself that "I live in a friendly, supportive universe that loves me, and wants me to be happy and succeed." Doing so will send out the initial wave with which everything else that occurs that day will resonate.

Place an image on your cell phone, computer, or other places that will represent a friendly universe to you. Maybe it could even be an image from Star Wars. What you send out this moment determines what is on its way back to you. Therefore, always calm yourself and do your best to "be happy now." If things start to become tense and confusing, it is even more important to do this.

Visualize Exactly What You Want

Your goal is to morph your reality to give you what you want. However, you've got to decide what you want. Perhaps you've been at a restaurant with a huge, detailed, extensive menu. The waiter is standing there, pencil in hand, ready to take your order. You may feel overwhelmed and even become speechless. It's okay to ask the waiter to come back because you need more time to think about what you want. This process is the same. Look at all the options, imagine them playing out realistically, and decide what would make you happy. Then place your order.

If what you want is different from what you already have, then take baby steps, working your way toward it one visualization at a time. After all, despite their powerful Jedi support, the rebels still had to whittle away at their huge goal little by little. This should always be a fun process, since you're mentally placing yourself where you want to be. It works especially well when you do it at the same time you're doing something else you enjoy. Remember that the signals you send out when you envision positive, emotionally gratifying scenarios, are the strongest of all.

Remain in the Mindset of Receiving

When the universe grants your wish, your desire is probably not going to materialize from thin air and appear at your feet like leprechaun gold. Instead, the universe will gradually swirl and shift a plethora of unseen variables around to eventually bring you what you want. It will manifest via synchronistic events. However, believe it or not, what you ask for may be presented—your wish come true right in front of you—but you might not notice it, and thereby accidentally let it fly away! To prevent that, you must constantly be open to receiving anything the universe provides that might lead you one step closer to your goal. Be mindful that the last part of "attraction" is "action," and you must be responsive to the opportunities that arise, even helping to stir them up yourself. A Jedi can feel the force flowing through him, so you must be a channel for the conditions that will allow manifestation to occur. Furthermore—though this seems counterintuitive to most people—you must give in order to receive. Since all good things must flow to you, the worst thing you can do is stop the flow by being a weak or inactive participant in the energy exchanges of life.

Give It Time

Just as a farmer does not constantly dig up his seed to see if it is growing, you must have trust that your seed has been properly planted and all is proceeding well, although out of your direct sight. Your main concerns should be keeping your thoughts trained on what you want. Imagine beating a pathway through the weeds, toward a goal. The more you go down that pathway, the clearer it will become, and the more quickly and easily you will reach the ultimate goal. Repetition is your friend.

In order to manifest things as quickly as possible, you must continually remain aware of inspiration and opportunities. Do not try to force them, since that will not work. If you simply remain open to them while mentally working toward your goal, they will find their way to you. If you patiently remain in the aware, receiving mindset, you will recognize and move on them at the perfect time with Jedi precision.

Avoid the Negative

This process began with you moving away from the negative. But at this stage, the negative will inevitably reappear, tempting you back to your old ways. Again and again, villains such as Count Dooku employed this trick. That is why you must continue to avoid the negative. To do this effectively, you must draw on a positive memory bank. This means you take the time to think of some specific memories and scenarios that you know will make you feel good.

You might already do this and not even realize it. A lot of people dread going to the dentist, for example. Maybe when you go to the dentist, your fear makes you feel unpleasant. While your teeth are being picked or the drill is running, you imagine yourself in a much nicer environment. A positive memory bank is your secret weapon to shift your mind toward the positive, optimistic energies you need to project. Yoda tells Luke to remain calm and at peace. These thoughts you draw upon should help you achieve and maintain that state of mind during the most challenging scenarios you encounter.

Surround Yourself with Daily Reminders

We live in a world full of marketers, salespeople, politicians, and others who will try to manipulate you by instilling fear or a sense of lack in your life. Every product or agenda that is sold is based on convincing you that you do not have what is needed in your life. The purpose is to convince you to submit to their needs so your problem can be solved. In order to combat this, you must produce your own, customized, personalized, positive little ad campaign, targeted only at yourself. This means posting affirmations in places you will notice them, such as your mirrors, refrigerator, steering wheel, or above your bed.

In order for them to work effectively, always word them positively. If you remind yourself, "I will not fall off this tightrope," your brain will respond more strongly to the part that says, "fall off this tightrope" than the part that says, "I will not." As Yoda cautions Luke, don't use weak words like "try." Not only must you word your affirmations positively, pairing them with your good feelings about what is heading your way, but they must always feel honest to you. The goal is for these reminders to connect with you on a realistic level. By thinking about what is realistic for you, at any given time, you will give your brain the confidence it needs to send out the strongest signals.

Understand the Principles of Perfect Balance

Do not be frightened or unpleasantly surprised to see your world begin to change before your eyes. As you alter your reality, some things must break down so that others can be born. Whenever one door closes, another opens, and vice versa. Let this process be exciting for you. Many people stagnate in the same conditions year after year. You, on the other hand, are taking hold of your life and the reality you will experience. You are moving things forward in a positive way. Be happy to see the old guard in your life crumble away so that new energy and circumstances can arrive. This is what you wanted!

As we know from science, energy cannot be created or destroyed; it simply changes form. Now, you are at the helm of how that form is remolded. Rest assured that if you sincerely project positive, loving, happy wishes, then bad results cannot come from those wishes. Ironically, even Darth Vader, despite all his bad actions, eventually brought balance to the Force by the power of his good actions. Luke and Leia were born out of love, and that love was once again proven when Vader destroyed the Emperor. You may never know exactly how things will turn out, but you can make the most of your efforts by considering your relationship to the entire universe, including all the people within.

Remember the Mirror Effect

Most people grow up feeling primarily passive; as a result, they are often victimized. However, as an adult, when you realize that the world around you is often just a mirror of what you are sending out, you are given a wonderful opportunity. Your mind is a projector, sending out an image, and the people around you are often screens for that projector. Instead of jumping to the conclusion that someone or something else bears responsibility for your problems, accept the power you have. It is the only power that should be important to you.

This was illustrated during Luke's training exercise when he found his own face inside Darth Vader's mask in the cave on Dagobah. If your personal experience happens inside your head, then maybe you should focus on repainting the picture in your head to alter the outward projection. Sometimes this can result in near-magical transformations of the people and events around you. As Socrates so often stressed, *Know thyself.*

Court the Universe Every Day

This is one of the most important parts of the process. You must mentally court the universe the way you would want to be courted. Whether or not you believe the universe is a living, conscious being that cares about your attitude toward it, if you *behave* as though it is, it will *also behave* as though it is. When you think of the universe, and how it sees you, use the same good manners you might in front of anyone for whom you have enormous respect. This also means not coming across as a needy, whiny, self-obsessed person. Nobody likes that kind of behavior, and you will quickly find that it is ineffective. It is your sense of calm, benevolence, and trust that will allow you to have a good time on this roller coaster ride called life.

You will be amazed by how much progress you can make by smiling. Smile at yourself. Smile at others. Smile at the sky and any time you see an impressive spectacle of nature. We are all part of nature. Even if you are reading this book on a smelly subway in a big city, you are still part of a quiet forest in the alpine mountains.

It doesn't mean the environments are equally pleasant to you, but you can appreciate them both as creations within the same grand system. The universe is constantly trying to speak with you, if you will only pay attention to its expressions in all the things around you. Therefore, treat everything within and around you like a massive handful of I Ching coins constantly falling into place. This is how Luke Skywalker put aside his targeting computer, yet sent the crucial shots into the Darth Star. He was able to sense the targeting through his mutually respectful relationship with the Force.

Beware of the Dark Side

Because the Law of Attraction behaves as a law, it is indifferent toward human opinions of "good" or "bad." This means that even the Force can be used effectively by evil people, like Darth Vader and the Emperor, in addition to the good. There is strong evidence that Adolf Hitler was a real-world example of a Jedi who aligned himself with the dark side to accomplish astounding feats of evil. And yet, despite his wicked achievements, Hitler found, just like Vader and the Emperor, that what you project will always come back to you. As a skilled practitioner in the ways of the Force, you must be especially discerning between the light and the dark. Otherwise, you might unwittingly become a pawn in someone else's dark agenda, just as Palpatine manipulated Anakin.

You must especially beware of those who focus on persuading and tempting you with isolated intellectual arguments, even if they try to tie them in to an emotional part of your life. Regardless of what situation you end up in, you should do fine if you always follow the Golden Rule: "Do unto others as you would have them do unto you." This is the surest way to lean in the right direction.

You will often have to judge others and their agendas to sense the truth. When it comes to evaluating other people and circumstances seriously, you would be wise to reserve judgment or knowledge until stringent parameters are met. Get as close to the source of gossip as you can before making crucial decisions that will impact others.

Do Your Best to Grasp the Latest Science

We live in an age full of scientifically produced wonders. The more you understand about science, the more you will be able to explain your new life to others, and the more confident you will feel in the practical reality of the Force and your ability to use it.

People have a tendency to stick with what they know according to how it was when they first learned it. This is especially the case with mainstream scientists and educators. Because of that, we are surrounded by a great deal of old-fashioned thinking about how the world works. However, it is important for you to be an open explorer and learner, staying abreast of the latest scientific findings, particularly as they directly relate to the mind-body-environment relationship. Data regarding the double-slit experiments, the placebo effect, black holes, dark matter, and dark energy are shattering old paradigms and reaffirming the potential for your mind to influence the universe in which you live.

While you might, and should, find this exhilarating, the old guard will fight tooth and nail to preserve their own relevance—especially in these fast-changing times. There is more and more evidence accruing every day indicating that the fantastic magic of the quantum world can make an impact on this macro world in which you live. Even Nobel Prizes have been awarded to scientists who have shown this. Those who are making true, practical headway in technology are those who embrace new and unfamiliar paradigms of data. We have found that our world is a holographic one, in which the Force connects us all. You, yourself, are a mentally active holographic representation, and so you are capable of impacting all those other holographic representations around you, no matter how bizarre, far away, inaccessible, or unobtainable they may seem. We are seeing how notions of science and spirituality have merged, and you must clearly understand the difference between science and spirituality, respecting both.

Noticing

One of my favorite books is *The Mothman Prophecies*, written by John Keel in 1975. It is a story rife with bizarre richness. Keel traveled to Point Pleasant, West Virginia, in 1966 and 1967, covering reports of a tall, dark, winged, humanoid creature terrorizing the people of the small, rural township. At that time, a whole host of other paranormal weirdness, including UFOs, men in black, and poltergeist phenomena was rampant in the region. Keel's book was turned into the creepy 2002 film *The Mothman Prophecies*, starring Richard Gere and Laura Linney. There is a particular moment in that movie that always stands out in my mind.

John Klein (Richard Gere), and his wife Mary are in a car. It's night and Mary is driving. She suddenly swerves to avoid an apparition shaped like a large moth, which appears in front of the vehicle. Though John is fine, Mary dies from the accident. He finds an assortment of drawings Mary had created depicting the weird creature and becomes obsessed with learning what this ominous being was. After finding that people have seen these eerie, shadowy, winged beings all throughout history, he is eventually led to an expert on the subject named Alexander Leek. "What you really want to know is, *Why you?*" says Leek.

"Yes," responds Klein.

"You noticed them, and they noticed that you noticed them," says Leek.

When you use the Law of Attraction every day, and start paying more attention to the connections in your life, you will see those connections begin to materialize even more plainly and quickly. Eventually, every day will be a dazzling display of pieces falling into place almost geometrically, like blocks guided on a Tetris screen. The very fact that you are looking for those connections energizes them, and causes them to manifest. Sometimes they will involve profound changes, and other times they will just occur to make your day a little better, or bring you something you wanted. I'll give you a personal example.

Twenty years ago, I enjoyed a fine bottle of French white wine at a nice restaurant in Asheville. I mentioned to my wife, Lauren, that I'd like to buy that label again. I only alluded to it in passing, but every time she remembered to look for it at a wine shop, it was not in stock. A few months ago, we were staying at a hotel near Asheville. As we were driving down the road, I saw a wine shop that was closed. For some reason, that bottle of French wine popped into my mind, and I said aloud, "I wonder if they have that label?"

When we arrived at the hotel, I needed to visit the office. The lady at the front desk said to me, out of the blue, "There's a new wine shop that opened next door. The fellow who owns it just came by and dropped off some fliers. Would you like one?" Of course I took one, and realized it was only open for another fifteen minutes. Lauren and I headed over and browsed quickly. In minutes, I heard a voice say my name. I turned to find a man walking from the back, apparently the owner. "Do I know you?" I asked. He chuckled and told me that twenty years ago he had been my waiter at that restaurant, and remembered who I was. Yes, he recalled the exact wine. And yes, it was on a shelf about ten feet away. I bought that wine, and we drank it with awe that night. I just kept thinking about how powerful the Law of Attraction is, even when it comes to the little comforts in life.

Feeling the Force

In the Star Wars series, a Jedi can frequently detect the presence of another Jedi, even from far away. This is because a Jedi has become a refined conduit, around which the often chaotic energies of life are able to organize. Just as a random spread of iron filings forms a nice pattern around a magnet, the Force around a Jedi coalesces into a meaningful flow.

If you rub a plastic comb on a piece of wool and build up a strong electrostatic charge, you can feel that charge against your skin. It makes your individual strands of hair stand up and move, pulled toward the charged comb as you wave it around. As you learn to master the Force, your entire bio-frequency is attaining a higher, more pronounced posture. That frequency, through sympathetic resonance, will affect all substances and people around you.

The human body is an electrical machine that produces several watts and carries thousands of volts. Every time your heart beats, a field—a unique fingerprint of your bio-field at that moment—pulsates around you. You can affect the mood of a room based on how other people, acting as antennae, receive your energy. This is from a Newtonian perspective; that energy is also detectable on a quantum level, not limited by space and time. This might help explain why precognition, the ability to see the future, is often associated with the Jedi. If you are in touch with the energy of people and situations around you, you can feel the direction in which things are going.

In *Episode V: The Empire Strikes Back*, Luke holds a handstand as he trains on Dagobah, lifting objects around him with his mind. "Yes," Yoda praises him. "Through the Force, things you will see. Other places. The future . . . the past. Old friends long gone." Luke is suddenly disrupted by a vision that his friends are in trouble at Cloud City. "It is the future you see," says Yoda. Luke asks Yoda if they will die. Yoda closes his eyes for a moment. "Difficult to see," he replies. "Always in motion is the future." Just as Yoda suggests, as you develop your Force abilities, you are frequently in a position to change future outcomes by using your influence through the Force. "If you leave now, help them you could . . ." Yoda says.

When Yoda closes his eyes to peer into the future, we imagine he is engaging in a moment of introspection. You must also take time to introspect, to peer inside yourself, every day. There are a number of ways to do this, depending on what puts your mind most at ease. Some people prefer to use traditional meditation techniques such as closing your eyes and focusing on breathing deeply as you mentally repeat an abstract word or mantra. Others may go to a special place, whether inside their home or outside, for a moment of calm. You might listen to a piece of music. I enjoying playing various musical instruments *without* an audience, since they are tools to remove my mind from distractions.

You should also considering wearing an object—a necklace or ring—that will remind you of your connection to the universe. If you want to keep its meaning private, think of a public explanation for it but have another meaning you keep only for yourself. Though many people get tattoos of things that remind them to introspect, it is good to have an object that you can put on and take off, so that the repetitive handling of the object affects you subconsciously. Having moments alone to introspect should humble you, as you feel the magnitude of life and are grateful that you are a part of this magnificence. Mother Teresa once said, "If you are humble, nothing will touch you, neither praise nor disgrace, because you know what you are." See your time in introspection as time intended to realign you with the Force and instill confidence. Understand that all the wonder of the universe was here before you had this life and will be here once this life is over. Thus you should simply relax and trust in the present experience to take you where you need to go.

Be Self-Aware

Self-awareness is one of the key factors that seems to separate humans from other animals. We look into a mirror and understand that we are seeing ourselves. Most animals do not make this connection. Some creatures such as apes and dolphins are gaining ground in this area, but nothing compares to the self-awareness of mature humans. This is one reason why mirrors are such a wonderful place to post your affirmations. Through the years, I have posted a number of different notes and reminders on the mirrors of my home, but there is one that always stays the same. It is at the very top. It is simply "Thank you." This simple phrase, present in all cultures, accomplishes much.

- First off, it is a humble acknowledgement that you are being helped. This places you in a position of mutual respect with the universe.
- Second, it is entirely positive, sending only pure waves of goodness out to be projected back to you.
- Third, it is a great equalizer of humans, since both a poor person and a rich person should be grateful for something.

I always smile when I see "Thank you" on my mirror, and I say "Thank you" out loud to the universe whenever possible. I find that whatever is happening at that moment, I always immediately see *something* for which to truly be thankful. It is even important to be thankful for your mistakes. Because of them, you have learned. Bad things are often there so that you learn the difference between good and bad.

Masaru Emoto was a Japanese researcher who claimed that human consciousness has an effect on the molecular structure of water. He died in 2014, but I was able to interview him, through a translator, on my weekly radio program, *Speaking of Strange*. Emoto's work was featured in the movie *What the Bleep Do We Know!?* He would take water specimens and subject them to different words, such as "I love you" or "thank you," and then freeze them and photograph them. He would also expose other samples to phrases such as "I hate you" or "you're ugly" and do the same thing. He believed that water is the "blueprint for our reality"; therefore, emotional energies and vibrations can change its physical structure. Again and again, his photographs showed that water subjected to positive thoughts produced beautiful, snowflake-like designs. Water subjected to negativity produced broken, jagged, distorted shapes. Obviously, this kind of work is considered pseudoscience by the mainstream, partially because it involves the selective process of choosing samples for demonstration purposes. However, the concept here is fascinating. We know that saying positive things such as "thank you" makes a positive impact on reality, so I would not be surprised if it can be visualized this way as well. And don't forget that a human body consists of up to 70 percent water.

The Power of Words

Saying positive things to others and to the universe is a major aspect of projecting the kind of energy you want returned to you. This concept is at the heart of chanting magical spells. Yet, for many years, linguistic experts have cautioned us against even using the term "Law of Attraction." My friend Dale Allen Hoffman is an expert on the Aramaic language and its connection to mysticism. On one of his CDs, *Enana: Living from the I Am*, he points out that saying you want to attract something implies you do not already have it. But, he says, manifesting (or materializing the obvious) is about acknowledging that it already exists (as does everything in the universe), so you needn't separate yourself from the object of your desire by indicating you don't already have that object. It is absolutely true that everything you want is already there somewhere. But you may not have it in front of you this very moment. I can tell a hungry man that the food is already there in some metaphysical sense, but that alone will not physically fill his stomach. So remember that what you desire *is* there, but you still must take practical steps in order to bring it into your hands—thus attracting it. Using the Force is about taking practical steps to get solid results in your life.

Everything in your life has been attracted in some way. When you emerged from the womb, there were certain attributes attracted by your genes. Even if we, in some past life, chose the conditions of our birth, there still must have been a point in the distant past where we just came out, for the first time, the way we were. Each day, as you focus on being grateful, and then channeling that energy into the specific things you desire, the most important thing to avoid is fear.

Some biologists argue that this emotion, fear, is the single most important engine for evolutionary development. Fear is what initially energizes life forms to swim faster, run farther, and fly higher, to survive by being the best adapted. This no doubt plays a huge role in the evolution of the animal kingdom. However, developments in biological evolution are said to come from mutations. These are conditions in which things do not function according to the normal plan.

In his 2007 documentary *Encounters at the End of the World*, Werner Herzog profiles the wonders and eccentricities of people and places in Antarctica. As he films a colony of penguins at one point, Herzog shows that most of a group waddles off to the open feeding grounds on the water. Another penguin returns back to the heart of the colony. But there is one particular penguin that does neither. He just stands there, solitary, in the middle of the vast whiteness. Then, without explanation, he turns and treks off toward the icy mountains more than forty miles away. The penguin scientist on location is Dr. David Ainley. Herzog says, as we watch this penguin disappear into the vast, distant landscape, "Dr. Ainley explained that, even if he caught him, and brought him back to the colony, he would immediately head right back for the mountains. But why?" Next, Herzog shows footage of another such penguin, waddling around near a base camp. His voice-over explains, "One of these disoriented or deranged penguins showed up at the New

Harbor diving camp, already some 80 kilometers away from where it should be . . . And here, he's heading off into the interior of the vast continent. With 5,000 kilometers ahead of him, he is heading toward certain death."

Let us imagine that, over the years, a million different penguins, struck by some mysterious motivation, will inexplicably turn and head into those mountains, but only a handful survive. Those that survive may do so because they have some superior physical trait, born of a mutation and passed along to their descendants, which allows them to step onto a different rung of evolution. Yet, the mutation surely seemed to begin in the brains of all the penguins who disregarded fear.

Whether or not we consider this a symptom of stupidity, insanity, or some suicidal sense of adventure, this kind of scenario continually plays throughout all of Mother Nature. There is a selection of every population that always marches to the beat of a different drummer. Humans are perhaps the greatest examples of this. We have now gone to almost every chunk of dirt on this planet, the bottom of the ocean, and even the moon! When I stand at the Smithsonian National Air and Space Museum, in Washington, D.C. and peer into the "tin cans" that astronauts squeezed into in the 1960s, I have no doubt those men had a lot in common with the penguins. However it arises, lack of fear is what drives us to achieve more. You exist, in your present human form, because humans before you proceeded without fear. Now you can relax, enjoying the fruits of their labors, and realize that you, too, should throw fear aside. You live in a society spilling over with opportunities, and fear can no longer stand in your way.

The Star Wars saga is essentially about overcoming fear. It was fear that drove Anakin to give in to the promises of the Emperor.

When he gave into the fear that his wife might die, she did. It was fear that Luke Skywalker had to overcome to face off against the most powerful foes in the galaxy. Because Luke did not give in to his fear, things turned out his way.

The lesson here is clear. Any moment you are feeling fear, switch your thoughts elsewhere, then act if you need to remove yourself from danger. Just as gratitude attracts more things for which to be grateful, fear attracts more things to fear. Acknowledge fear, but do not be afraid. You will receive back whatever you put out.

There are some who may look at using the Force as mere wishful thinking. This could not be further from the truth. To simply toss out a wish is sloppily throwing a wobbly Frisbee into a storm. Using the Force is a specific technique, and you must follow all aspects of that technique in order to gain results. Everything that has a lasting impact on life requires some structure; otherwise it will simply collapse. The techniques in this book and others you will read on the subject will reinforce the structure of your mind, providing a platform on which your projected thought forms can launch and be sustained by your mission control. Yet, the techniques should feel extremely natural to you. It's not like beginning a new diet or instituting a regime to practice a new instrument. You should feel that everything you've read in this book resonates with you on a natural, logical level. The method feels right because it works.

I have sometimes wondered, while watching the Star Wars movies, why more people in the galaxy aren't clamoring to be Jedi. You'd think there would be a line around the block of people filling out applications to be trained by Yoda. Here on Earth, we would turn it into a reality TV show! You might say it's because being a Jedi may be cool in times of peace, but nobody wants to really raise a lightsaber to Darth Vader, Count Dooku, or General Grievous. That is surely part of it, and yet I feel there is a deeper reason, one that resonates with us right here on Earth.

Fluid Reality

The Jedi mentality, and the Force, show us that reality is a fluid and impressionable thing. For those who have creative minds, this is the most exciting concept imaginable. However, most of the world's population is not that creative. For them, the idea of a fluid reality is as scary and disorienting as if someone were to jerk the floor out from underneath them. Therefore, most of the people on this planet create constructs. They work together to envision spiritual frameworks based upon physical frameworks (this is why ancient Europeans attributed thunder and lightning to the power of the angry god Thor). Generation after generation, they pass this model down. It survives because, if it is to change, someone must change it. But nobody wants to step up and do that, especially since most people don't have any idea *how* to do that. This is your opportunity to trail-blaze a new way of thinking. It begins by understanding that you, yourself, are not a pawn of creation, but an author of creation.

This book has dealt with some of the most complex issues known to humankind. Perhaps the most difficult question is why do we exist at all? Though no one can answer that question, here is something to consider: Perhaps we are here because the universe needed an outside perspective on itself. If so, that means you are granted a very special power. You are able to not only explore what this creation is but even adjust and tweak it with your own thoughts, suggestions, and mental projections. Imagine that! Perhaps this whole time, as people leave snippy comments on web pages, they could instead be directing their intentions into the fabric of space-time to actually morph the world to their liking.

Making a Difference

Regardless of whether or not you are here to change the world at large, there is no doubt that you can have an astounding impact on your life and those lives around you. Just as the Star Wars Jedi were bastions of hope in their galaxy, you must be a confident ambassador for the Force to your friends and family. You should be a living example of what can be accomplished when using the Force, and be patiently willing to share your experiences and wisdom with others. When it comes to this topic, we should remember the words of a famous broadcaster.

Larry King is best known as the host of CNN's *Larry King Live* from 1985 to 2010. During his career, he has interviewed thousands of people. My favorite quote by him is, "I never learned anything while I was talking." This could almost serve as an anthem to intelligence. To improve, you must acknowledge that there are worthy things in the universe outside yourself. When you talk to another person, you should always bear this in mind. Everyone you meet can teach you something. When you lay eyes on another person, think about why this individual has come into your life. Whether the person has been there for thirty years or thirty seconds, you apparently attracted that person into your life. It was so you could learn something from him or her, and share something with him or her. The universe is a gigantic place, thus you attracted each other to that spot at that time. Don't let it go to waste.

"Luke" is a form of "Lucas." I find it no coincidence that George Lucas named the young man exploring the Force *Luke*. There was a "Luke" 13,000 years ago . . . there was a "Luke" 2,000 years ago . . . there was a "Luke" born yesterday . . . and you are "Luke" this very moment. Even the ancient, ascended masters would say you now have everything you need. It's all right here before you. The mission is clear, and you—yes, *you*—are our only hope. Use the technique. Find happiness for yourself and show others how to do the same. You and I have attracted each other, at this time, to share in this message. Surely, there is a reason. Go now, and use the Force for good. As Obi-Wan said to young Luke Skywalker, "You've taken your first step into a larger world."

May the Force be with you, always.

About the Author

Joshua P. Warren published his first book at fifteen. He is now the author of almost twenty books, sold in various languages around the world. He is the syndicated host of the *Speaking of Strange* radio show and a correspondent for the *Coast to Coast AM* radio show (the largest overnight radio program in North America). He has appeared on the History Channel, National Geographic, Discovery, SyFy, Animal Planet, and TLC, and starred in the Travel Channel series *Paranormal Paparazzi*. He has also worked in feature films as a technical consultant for Warner Brothers. In 2004, he made the cover of the *Electric Space Craft* science journal for his work reproducing mysterious plasmas at his L.E.M.U.R. Lab. He also owns the Asheville Mystery Museum and leads popular tours in his hometown of Asheville, North Carolina. Warren's work has been recognized by CNN, Fox News, *Entertainment Weekly*, *Delta Sky*, the *New York Times*, *FHM*, and many other major publications. He created and owns the Sunshine Simple company, producing solar generators and clean energy alternatives for people around the world. As creator of the Wishing Machine project, he has helped thousands of people, around the world, change their lives in profound ways.

Warren is always in demand as a speaker. He was hired by the A&E television network to host and entertain executives and VIPs on a cruise through the Bermuda Triangle. He produced an all-day event at the esteemed Rhine Research Center and has been a featured speaker in hundreds of venues, including the North Carolina Center for the Advancement of Teaching, the International UFO Congress in Nevada and Arizona (the world's largest UFO event), the *RMS Queen Mary* GhostFest in California, the Chicago Ghost Conference, the South Carolina Crytozoology Society Conference, the Brown Mountain Lights Symposium, *George Noory Live*, Para-History Con in New York, and countless events for major medical and business clients at the Grove Park Inn resort and spa. He led an expedition to the Mayan pyramids in Central America, investigated the Tower of London, and co-hosted an expedition through Transylvania in Romania, conducting scientific tests at places where dramatic historic events occurred.

When he's not traveling, Warren generally divides his time between Asheville and Puerto Rico, where he directs the Bermuda Triangle Research Base. You can learn more about Warren, and see samples of his work and TV appearances, at *www.JoshuaPWarren.com*.

Index

used for evil, 142–43. *See also*
   Hitler, Adolf
Len, Dr. Hew, 84–85
Light. *See* Goodness (light)
Lightsabers, 46, 71, 172–73
Liminal life, 39–41
Lincoln, Abraham, 157
Look Homeward, Angel (Wolfe),
   190
Love
   power of forgiveness and, 30–32
   separation from, turning to the
      dark side and, 159
   success from, 105
Lucas, George, 10, 14, 17, 61, 148,
   166, 187, 211–12

M

Manifestation. *See also* Law of
   Attraction; Visualization
   affirmations for. *See* Daily
      reminders (affirmations)
   beginning process, 68
   going with the flow and, 57–58
   luck, work and, 56
   relaxing, then seizing, 74–77
   repetition for, 70–72
   sowing seeds of future, 68–69,
      76–77
   time required for. *See* Time, for
      manifestation/visualization
   trusting instincts, 75–77
   uniqueness of events, 68
   visualization steps, 46–52
The Millions Within (Neagle), 136–37
Mind
   affecting matter. *See* Mind,
      affecting matter
   animal instincts and, 21–22, 24–
      25, 124, 157
   conscious, 20
   controlling world inside, 121–22

   creating your own reality, 85–86
   happy pigs, Lincoln and, 157
   mindfulness and, 84–88
   objects originating in, 53
   prepared, chance and, 134–38
   preparing, to use Force, 191
   solipsism dangers, 86–87
   stilling thoughts, 39
   subconscious, 20–22
   telepathy and, 19, 53, 181
   as tuning fork, 20–21
   as ultimate tool, 133–34
   useless knowledge, gossip and,
      154–59
   visualizing with. *See* Visualization
Mind, affecting matter
   electron experiment showing,
      163–64
   object origins and, 53
   power over physical world, 44–46
   quantum entanglement and,
      164–66
   spooky action at a distance,
      164–66
   telekinesis, 52, 58, 71, 134
   tuning, controlling thoughts for,
      19–20
Mirror effect, 113–22, 196–97
   description of, 114–15
   projecting your reality and,
      114–15
   redirecting your focus and,
      115–18
   remembering, for using Force,
      196–97
   self-perception and, 114
   taking responsibility for how
      others treat you, 117–18
   unlearning perceived reality and,
      118–20
Money
   feeling abundance and, 58–59

getting what you wish for, 62–63

Money—*continued*

giving as basis of receiving, 59–63

how to receive, 63–64

materializing, 49

never enough, 63–64

overattachment to/greed, 60–61, 62–63

The Mothman Prophesies (Keel), 200–201

N

Neagle, David, 136–37

Necklace, reminding of universe connection, 202–3

Neediness, 128–31

Negativity (dark side), 139–60, 198–99. *See also* Evil; Fear; Hitler, Adolf

avoiding, 28–29, 79–88, 160, 194–95

beware of, 139–60, 198–99

bodily reactions to truth and, 146–47

buildup of, 26–28

calmness counteracting, 83

cost of, 143–44

Darth Vader's redemption from, 159

dealing with, 29–30

fear leading to, 139, 160

gossip and useless knowledge, 154–59

Han Solo taking action against, 144–45

harboring feelings of, 24–25

lack of positivity vs., 83–84

love, forgiveness overcoming, 30–32. *See also* Love

mindfulness to avoid, 84–88

mirror effect and, 113–22

neutrality of Force and, 65–66

parental figures and, 25–26

positive life moments eclipsing, 81–82

power of, 158–59, 160

power of words and, 206–10

rage and, 25

self-perception and, 114–15. *See also* Mirror effect

separation from love and, 159

slipping over to, 152

solipsism dangers, 86–87

strength of light vs., 148

subconscious mind and, 20–22

victimhood and, 87–88

vigilance against, 152–54

your "Emperor figure" and, 160

Newton, Sir Isaac, 20, 57, 182

Noticing (observing), power/ importance of, 187–88, 200–202

O

Opportunities

awareness of inspiration and, 72–74

chance, preparedness and, 134–38

relaxing, then seizing, 74–77

P

Parental figures, 25–26

Pasteur, Louis, 134

Patterns, looking for, 135–36

Peacefulness, 127–28

Penguins, role of fear and, 207–8

Pigs, happy, 157

Point of view/perspective

distorted, 157

good/bad as, 150, 151–52

importance of, 34

power of observation and, 187–88, 200–202

on universe, 34–39

Visualization, 43–53, 192–93. *See also* Manifestation

affirmations for. *See* Daily reminders (affirmations)

automatism and, 44

daily routine, 46–47

emotional, 48–49

experiment demonstrating, 44

happiness and, 48

manifestation through, 46–52

mind, world and, 44–46

repetition for, 70–72

size of steps for, 49–51

specificity guidelines, 51–52

as step to using Force, 192–93

time required for. *See* Time, for manifestation/visualization

Vitale, Dr. Joe, 46, 114

Voltaire, 17

W

Water, consciousness affecting, 205–6

Winfrey, Oprah, 15

Wisdom, knowledge and, 124–26

Wishing machines (radionics), 173–75

Wolfe, Thomas, 190

Words, power of, 206–10

Wormhole Brain Theory, 181

Worrying, reality of, 38

Y

Young, Thomas, 162